KOREAN FOR EVERY

COMPLETE SELF-STUDY PROGRAM

<BEGINNER LEVEL>

WITH EASY-TO-UNDERSTAND ILLUSTRATIONS!

PRONUNCIATION | WRITING | KOREAN ALPHABET
GRAMMAR | SPELLING | VOCABULARY | PRACTICE QUIZ

979-11-88195-96-1

BRIDGE EDUCATION

Ordering Information:
Quantity sales. Special discounts are available on quantity purchases by corporations, associations, and others.
For details, contact the publisher at the email address below.

marketing@newampersand.com

www.newampersand.com
14 13 12 11 10 / 10 9 8 7 6 5 4 3 2 1

TABLE OF CONTENTS

3 CONSONANTS & VOWELS

8 SYLLABLE STRUCTURE

13 SYLLABLE BLOCK TYPES

22 WRITING PRACTICE - CONSONANTS

42 WRITING PRACTICE - VOWELS

62 SENTENCE STRUCTURE

    63   Subject Marker - 이/가
    64   Topic Marker - 은/는
    69   Object Marker - 을/를
    71   Predicate

75 ADJECTIVES & CONJUGATION RULES

    76   Irregular ㅂ batchim adjective
    76   Irregular ㅎ batchim adjective
    77   Adjectives and their uses

80 Adverbs

    81   Rule # 1 하다 -> ˜게 / ˜히 Type
    81   Rule # 1-1 하다 -> ˜이/히 Type
    81   Rule # 1 Ausnahme Beispiel
    82   Rule # 2 ˜게-Type
    82   Rule # 3 ˜적으로
    82   Rule # 4: Never Changing Forms

86 IMITATING WORDS

90 KOREAN VERBS & CONJUGATION RULES

    92   Present
    94   Present Continuous
    96   Past
    98   Future
    100 Inquisitive Present
    102 Inquisitive Past
    104 Inquisitive Future
    106 Propositive

108 PASSIVE VERBS

    111 Stem + 어지다 / 아지다 / 지다 / 이다
    112 Stem + 히다 / 리다 / 기다
    113 Stem + 하다 / 되다 / 내다 / 나다

116 PLACES ˜에서 / 부터 & ˜ 까지

120 NUMBERS IN KOREAN

    123 Sino-Korean Numbers
    125 Pure Korean Numbers

132 TELLING TIME IN KOREAN

136 TYPES OF SENTENCES

    136 Explaining & Describing
    138 Negative / Negation 안 / ˜지 않다
    140 Choosing between options ˜이(나) / ˜거나
    142 Comparative ˜보다 & 더/덜
    144 Exclamative Sentence ˜구나! / ˜(ㄹ)수가!
    146 Wishing/Hoping ˜(으)면 좋겠다
    147 Resolution / Determination ˜아/어야 한다
    148 Permission˜아/어 도 된다 & ˜으(면) 안된다
    150 Reason ˜아/어서 / ˜기 때문에
    152 Possibility ˜ㄹ/을 수 있다 & ˜ㄹ/을 수 없다
    154 Despite˜지만
    156 Quote ˜(ㄴ/는)다고 / ˜았/었다고 / ˜ㄹ 거라고
    158 Guess ˜ㄹ/을/ㄴ/은 것 같다 / ˜었던 것 같다
    160 Condition / If ˜(으)면, ˜(ㄴ/는) 다면
    162 At The Same Time ˜(으)면서 / ˜며
    164 Nearly / Almost ˜ㄹ/을 뻔 했다
    166 Make / Let / Force ˜게 하다 / ˜ 게 해 주다 / ˜게 만들다

168 OTHER COMMON EXPRESSIONS

170 HONORIFICS

Every lesson comes with an audio track
recorded by a native Korean speaker!

Learn to speak and listen
accurately!

CONSONANTS & VOWELS

All right, guys! Let's start with the basics. The Korean alphabet system, Hangul, has **14** consonants and **10** vowels (along with **5** additional tense consonants and **11** double vowels).

Pay attention to the ones in colored rows. They appear to have **2** of the same base consonants (for example, "ㄲ" has two "ㄱ"s, and "ㄸ" has two "ㄷ"s, and so on). There are five of these, and they are called **tense consonants**, pronounced with a harder and stiffer sound.

So, having two of the same consonant makes it stronger, right? Hence the name tense consonants. If you're a Spanish speaker, you might have noticed that these sounds are similar to how "C," "T," and "P" are pronounced in Spanish. That is, "ㄲ" sounds similar to the "c" in "Corea," "ㄸ" sounds similar to the "t" in "tiburÓn," and "ㅃ" sounds similar to the "p" in "pollo."

🔊 **MP3 (1)**

AUDIO #1 Name	Pronunciation Initial / Final	English Approximation	Korean Example
ㄱ 기역 gi-yŏk	g / k	**good**	가수 **g**asu
ㄲ 쌍기역 ssang gi-yŏk	kk / k	**skin**	꿈 **kk**um
ㄴ 니은 ni-ŭn	n / n	**n**ano	노루 **n**oru
ㄷ 디귿 di-gŭt	d / t	**d**og	다리 **d**ari
ㄸ 쌍디귿 ssang di-gŭt	dd	**st**all	땀 **dd**am
ㄹ 리을 ri-ŭl	r / l	**r**oman	라면 **r**amyŏn
ㅁ 미음 mi-ŭm	m / m	**m**an	마법 **m**abŏp
ㅂ 비읍 bi-ŭp	b / p	**b**ean	보배 **b**obae
ㅃ 쌍비읍 ssang bi-ŭp	bb	**sp**it	빨리 **bb**ali
ㅅ 시옷 si-ot	s / t	**s**ing	소리 **s**ori
ㅆ 쌍시옷 ssang si-ot	ss	**s**ee	싸움 **ss**aum
ㅇ 이응 i-ŭng	silent / ng	**vowel sound**	아기 **a**gi
ㅈ 지읒 ji-ŭt	j / t	**j**am	자유 **j**ayu
ㅉ 쌍지읒 ssang ji-ŭt	jj	ha**ts**	짬뽕 **jj**amppong
ㅊ 치읓 chi-ŭt	ch / t	**ch**ange	최고 **ch**oego
ㅋ 키읔 ki-ŭk	k / k	**k**ing	커피 **k**ŏpi
ㅌ 티읕 ti-ŭt	t / t	**t**ime	타자 **t**aja
ㅍ 피읖 pi-ŭp	p / p	**p**rize	피로 **p**iro
ㅎ 히읗 hi-ŭt	h / t	**h**ome	해변 **h**aebyŏn

Are you wondering what it means by "Initial / Final" pronunciation? Don't worry! It's not as difficult as it may sound. Don't close the book and give up on your Korean study just yet. We'll get to the bottom of it after we cover the vowels.

🔊 **MP3 ⟨2⟩**

	Pronunciation	English Approximation	Korean Example
ㅏ	a	grandpa	자두 jadu
ㅑ	ya	see-ya	야구 yagu
ㅓ	ŏ	up	접시 jŏpsi
ㅕ	yŏ	young	명화 myŏnghwa
ㅗ	o	go	고무 gomu
ㅛ	yo	yogurt	교사 gyosa
ㅜ	u	root	우주 uju
ㅠ	yu	you	소유 soyu
ㅡ	ŭ	good	그림 gŭrim
ㅣ	i	hit	소리 sori
ㅔ	e	energy	세기 segi
ㅐ	ae	tablet	대박 daebak
ㅒ	yae	yes	얘기 yaegi
ㅖ	ye	yes	예복 yebok
ㅙ	oae	where	안돼 andwae
ㅞ	ue	quest	훼손 hweson
ㅚ	oe	wet	최고 choego
While ㅚ is ㅗ + ㅣ so "oi" seems right when followed the rules, it's pronounced as "oe", and it's not considered a "double vowel", either.			
ㅘ	wa	what	과일 gwail
ㅟ	wi	wisconsin	귀 gwi
ㅢ	ŭi	we	의자 ŭija
ㅝ	wŏ	wonder	권투 gwontu

Listen carefully and repeat!

The pronunciation symbols for vowels follow the McCune–Reischauer system. For more details of this system see:
http://mccune–reischauer.org

5

And the ones in colored rows are called **double vowels.** They are composed of two vowels that combine to create one sound.

Keep in mind that there are no English/Roman letters that perfectly describe these sounds. However, if we keep listening to the audio files and practicing, you will start to notice the differences!

ㅗ + ㅐ = 왜
[o]　　[e]　　[wae]

double vowels

One thing you might have noticed is how ㅐ / ㅔ practically sound the same, and ㅚ / ㅙ / ㅞ sound the same too! It might seem like a waste of ink, but their meanings are different when written. Until the late **20th** century, people used to distinguish the subtle differences in tongue and mouth position. However, these differences are seldom observed nowadays, and most Koreans can't tell them apart in terms of pronunciation (but they do have different meanings when written!).

ㅐ ㅔ

ㅚ ㅙ ㅞ

Phew!
I thought I was the only one who couldn't tell the difference.

And also pay close attention to the vowel ㅡ, which is transcribed using the phonetic symbol Ŭ. Although we used the word 'good' as an example, it doesn't fully replicate the sound. This vowel often poses difficulties for English speakers, primarily because there's no direct equivalent in the English alphabet. However, once you hear it, you will recognize it, so it's just a matter of getting used to it.

ㅡ

No problem!
If I keep practicing, I will be able to say it like a native Korean!

으 - 으 - 으!

I think I'm getting the hang of it!

PRACTICE QUIZ

**CIRCLE THE ONES THAT ARE
KOREAN CONSONANTS**

ㄱ	㇋	ㅉ	ニ	ㄷ
ㅕ	ㅗ	ㅠ	ㅌ	ㅜ
金	ㅎ	ㅇ	ㅖ	ㅐ
ㅝ	ㅁ	ㅂ	ㅜ	ㅅ
ㅋ	ㅟ	ㅘ	ㅚ	ㅙ

ANSWER : ㄱ,ㅉ,ㄷ,ㅎ,ㅇ,ㅁ,ㅂ,ㅅ,ㅋ

**CIRCLE THE ONES THAT ARE
KOREAN VOWELS**

ŋ	六	ㅏ	ニ	ㅜ
ㅁ	ㅗ	ㅛ	ㅌ	J
ひ	ㅎ	ㅂ	ㅖ	が
士	ㅓ	ㅅ	ㅇ	ㅆ
ㅋ	ㅟ	ㅘ	ㅚ	乂

ANSWER : ㅏ,ㅜ,ㅗ,ㅖ,ㅓ,ㅟ,ㅘ

The following letters are not in the correct order. Write down their numbers in correct alphabetical order.

1	2	3	4	5
나	마	라	차	사

6	7	8	9	10
자	가	아	하	카

11	12	13	14
바	타	파	다

ANSWER : 7 – 1 – 14 – 3 – 2 – 11 – 5 – 8 – 6 – 4 – 10 – 12 – 13 – 9

SYLLABLE STRUCTURE

As promised, let's talk about initial/final consonants! In Korean, a consonant(s) and a vowel are combined to create a syllable block, which consists of an initial consonant (chosŎng), a medial vowel (jungsŎng), and an optional final consonant (jongsŎng), known as batchim. To form a syllable block, you need at least one consonant and one vowel.

Let's take the word 소리 sori ("sound") as an example.

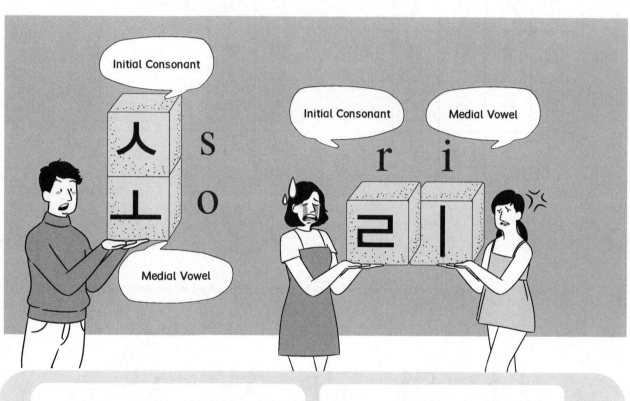

At this point, you might have noticed that the position of the vowel is different in the two syllables 소 / 리.

Sorry (pun intended), but that's just how the rules are, and there's no easy way around it. So, it's best to get used to it. The rules are as follows:

ㅏ ㅑ ㅓ ㅕ ㅐ ㅣ ㅒ ㅖ ㅔ

아 야 어 여 애 이 얘 예 에

These **9** vowels are positioned to the right side of a consonant. By the way, when a vowel is spoken by itself, ㅇ , which is silent, is always placed as a placeholder.

ㅗ ㅛ ㅜ ㅠ ㅡ ㅚ ㅟ ㅢ ㅘ ㅝ ㅙ ㅞ

오 요 우 유 의 외 위 의 와 워 왜 웨

And these **12** vowels are positioned underneath a consonant. We'll assist you in memorizing them through intensive training throughout the book!

Going back to our example, 소리, each syllable block consists of one consonant and one vowel, and does not have the optional final consonant, batchim.

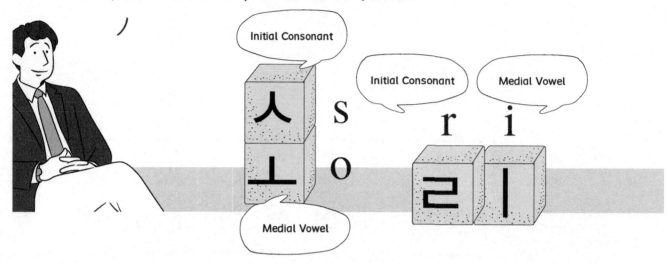

To put it simply, batchim refers to the last or final consonant of a word that ends with a consonant. For example, in English, the word "foot" has a final consonant of "t," and "sap" has a final consonant of "p." On the other hand, the word "employee" does not have a final consonant because it ends with a vowel.

Korean follows a similar pattern but with different graphical representation.

So let's try this one — 죽 juk ("porridge")

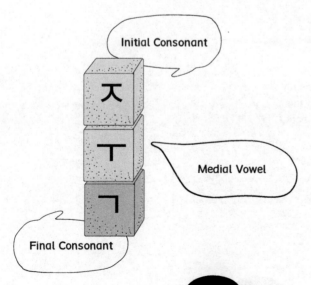

As you can see, the consonant ㄱ comes at the bottom to serve as the final consonant.

Notice that the vowel ㅜ is placed underneath the consonant ㅈ.

The rule we learned just a page ago is Initial Consonant – Vowel – Final Consonant (batchim).

How about another one? 각 gak ("angle")

In this case, the vowel ㅏ is placed to the right side of the initial consonant ㄱ, and the final consonant ㄱ is placed underneath the medial vowel.

Here's a tip: the final consonant (batchim) is always positioned underneath a vowel, regardless of whether it's a right-side type vowel or an underneath-type vowel.

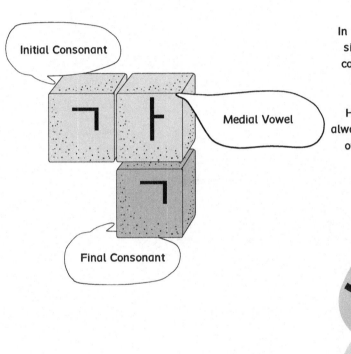

Initial Consonant

Medial Vowel

Final Consonant

Initial Consonant

vowel

batchim

ATLAS

Oh, and the word "batchim" means "to support / hold up." So, just picture it holding a consonant and a vowel, like the Titan god Atlas carrying the heavens upon his shoulders.

PRACTICE QUIZ

Which of the following has its parts named _incorrectly_?

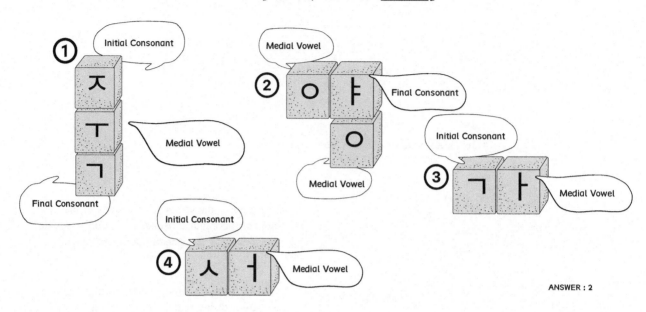

ANSWER : 2

Which of the following words don't have a batchim, or a final consonant?

죽 마 감 손 은

ANSWER : 마

The following words are incomplete. Please insert the correct consonants, vowels, and batchim!

hak gyo (school)   in gan (human)   go yang i (kitty)

gang a ji (puppy)   mul go gi (fish)   son mok si gye (wrist watch)

ANSWER :
학교 / 인간 고양이
강아지 / 물고기 / 손목시계

12

SYLLABLE BLOCK TYPES

> I know. What the heck is a **double FC**? Don't panic! It's simply a final consonant formed by combining two consonants, similar to double vowels. It's actually quite simple once you become familiar with it. We will discuss them in more detail later on.

IC = Initial Consonant
V = Media Vowel
FC = Final Consonant

IC + V

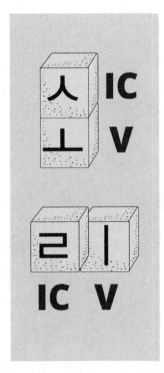

IC + V + FC

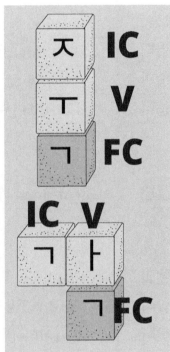

IC + V + DOUBLE FC

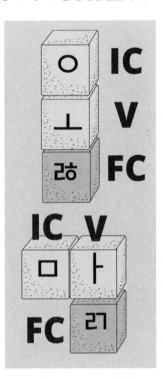

Okay, I'm sure you have a clear understanding of what a final consonant (batchim) is, right?

In case you haven't noticed, our previous example 각 has the same consonant ㄱ as both the initial and final consonant, but it is transcribed with different alphabets ('g' and 'k', respectively).

Remember the alphabet chart? I mentioned that the consonants can be used as either an initial or a final consonant (batchim), and their pronunciation may vary depending on how they are used.

	Name	Pronunciation Initial / Final	English Approximation	Korean Example
ㄱ	기역 gi-yŏk	g / k	good	가수 gasu

13

Consonant	Initial Consonant Sound	Final Consonant Sound	When Followed By A Consonant		When Followed By A Vowel	
ㄱ	g	k	책과	chaek-kkwa [꽈]	책이	chae-gi [기]
ㅋ	k		부엌과	buŏk-kkwa [꽈]	부엌에	buŏ-ke [케]
ㄲ	kk		깎다	kkak-dda [따]	깎아	kka-kka [까]
ㄴ	n	n	손과	son-gwa	손이	so-ni [니]
ㄷ	d	t	쏟다	ssot-dda [따]	쏟아	sso-da [다]
			when followed by a vowel ㅣ (i), it's sometimes pronounced as ㅈ (j)		쏟이	sso-ji [지]
ㅌ	t		끝단	ggŭt-ddan [딴]	끝에	ggŭ-te [테]
			when followed by a vowel ㅣ (i), it's sometimes pronounced as ㅊ (ch)		끝이	ggŭ-chi [치]
ㅅ	s		옷과	ot-kkwa [꽈]	옷이	o-si [시]
ㅆ	ss		있다	it-dda [따]	있어	i-ssŏ [쏘]
ㅈ	j		찾다	chat-dda [따]	찾아	cha-ja [자]
ㅊ	ch		꽃과	kkot-kkwa [꽈]	꽃이	kko-chi [치]
ㅎ	h		넣다	nŏt-ta [타]	넣어	nŏ-ŏ [어]
ㄹ	r	l	말과	mal-gwa	말이	ma-ri [리]
ㅁ	m	m	솜과	som-gwa	솜이	so-mi [미]
ㅂ	b	p	집과	jip-kkwa [꽈]	집이	ji-bi [비]
ㅍ	p		잎과	ip-kkwa [꽈]	잎이	i-pi [피]
ㅇ	silent	ng	콩과	kong-gwa	콩이	kong-i [이]

Looking at the above chart will visually help you understand how a consonant is pronounced differently when used as an initial consonant and as a final consonant (batchim).

Rule: There are only seven sounds for a final consonant, and they are k, n, t, l, m, p, ng, as explained in the chart.

Now, take a close look at what happens when a final consonant is followed by a vowel.
It is transferred to the position of the ㅇ in the vowel.

Consonant	Initial Consonant Sound	Final Consonant Sound	**2** When Followed By A Consonant		When Followed By A Vowel	
ㄱ	g		책과	chae**k-kk**wa [꽈]	책이	chae-**gi**
ㅋ	k	k	부엌과	buŏ**k-kk**wa [꽈]	부엌에	buŏ-**ke**
ㄲ	kk		깎다	kka**k-dd**a [따]	깎아	kka-**kka**
ㄴ	n	n	손과	son-gwa	손이	so-**ni**

1

Just think of it this way: we learned that syllables have a ㅇ as a placeholder when written by itself (e.g., 아, 어, 여, etc.). So, the final consonant of a syllable right before it takes the place of the placeholder.

솜 som + 이 i

the final consonant m comes in place of ㅇ, the vowel place holder,

솜↗이 Thus pronounced as [소미] so-mi.

Same goes for 부엌 buŏk, when followed by a vowel 에 e,

부엌 buŏk + 에 e

the final consonant k comes in place of ㅇ, the vowel place holder,

부엌↗에 Thus pronounced as [부어케] buŏ-ke.

When followed by a consonant, note that the sound of the following consonant gets affected,

batchim ㄱ (k) + following syllable ㄱ (g) = ㄲ
instead of 책과 [chaek-gwa] (x) [chaek-kkwa] (o) <- becomes a tense sound.

Final Consonant Batchim		Following Consonant Sound		Affected Sound
ㄱ (k) ㅋ (k) ㄲ (k) ㄷ (t) ㅌ (t) ㅅ (t) ㅆ (t) ㅈ (t) ㅊ (t) ㅂ (p) ㅍ (p)	+	ㄱ (g) ㄷ (d) ㅂ (b) ㅅ (s) ㅈ (j)	=	ㄲ (kk) ㄸ (dd) ㅃ (bb) ㅆ (ss) ㅉ (jj)

ㅎ is a unique one. Though it belongs to the (t) category,
it affects the following ㄱ (g) and ㄷ (d) differently. Just memorize these differences.

Final Consonant Batchim		Following Consonant Sound		Affected Sound
ㅎ (t)	+	**ㄱ (g)** **ㄷ (d)** ㅂ (b) ㅅ (s) ㅈ (j)	=	**ㅋ (k)** **ㅌ (t)** ㅃ (bb) ㅆ (ss) ㅉ (jj)

Lastly, the colored consonants retain their original initial consonant sound when followed by a vowel.
The only exceptions are ㅎ and ㅇ, which do not carry over and only the vowel is pronounced.

Consonant	Initial Consonant Sound	Final Consonant Sound	Example		When Followed By A Vowel	
ㅎ	h	t	넣다	nŏt-ta [타]	넣어	nŏ-ŏ
ㅇ	silent	ng	콩과	kong-gwa	콩이	kong-i

A few more examples to help you understand:

ㅎ	h	t	닿다	reach	dat-ta [타]	닿아	da-a
ㅇ	silent	ng	망과	net	mang-gwa	망이	mang-i

According to the rule, 닿다 dat-ta should sound [다타], but in real life,
it's frequently pronounced as dat-dda [다따].

 **MP3 〈4〉**

Now, in addition to the list of final consonants we learned, there are special types of consonants called double final consonants 〈겹받침 gyeopbatchim〉. There are **11** of them.

Consonant	Representative Sound	Example		When Followed By A Vowel	
ㄳ	k	넋과	nŏk-kkwa [넉꽈]	넋이	nŏk-si [시]
ㄺ		읽다	ik-dda [익따]	읽어	il-gŏ [거]
ㄵ	n	앉다	an-dda [안따]	앉아	an-ja [자]
ㄼ ●		넓다	nŏl-dda [널따] ●	넓이	nŏl-bi [비]
ㄽ	l	외곬	oe-gol [외골]	외곬이	oe-gol-si [시]
ㄾ ●		핥다	hal-dda [할따] ●	핥아	hal-ta [타]
ㅀ		닳다	dal-ta [달타]	닳아	da-ra [라]
ㅄ	p	없다	ŏp-dda [업따]	없이	ŏp-si [시]
ㄿ		읊다	ŭp-dda [읍따]	읊어	ŭl-pŏ [퍼]
ㄻ	m	삶다	sam-dda [삼따]	삶아	sal-ma [마]
ㄶ	n	많다	man-ta [만타]	많아	ma-na [나]

Note that for L sounds, ㄼ and ㄾ affect the following consonant to become a tense sound. If they followed the general rule where only the first part of the double batchim is pronounced, it should be 핥다 –> 할다 [hal–da] and the following consonant should not become a tense sound. However, these are exceptions.

In general, they follow the rules we learned, but for visual learners, let me break them down.

Let's take 읽 as an example. As you can see, the double final consonant ㄺ consists of two consonants combined: ㄹ (l) + ㄱ (k). They follow the general rules where the initial consonant sound replaces the placeholder ㅇ. But there are two consonants! Which one goes in there? It's easy!

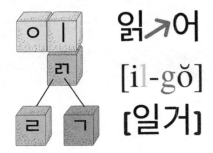

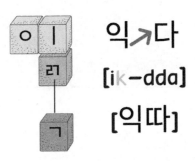

When followed by a vowel, the first part is pronounced, and the second part goes into the ㅇ!

When followed by a consonant, the representative sound is pronounced, and it affects the following consonant, following the rules we covered a few pages ago.

Congratulations, guys! You've come a long way!

That covers the fundamental elements of the Korean alphabet, Hangul, including pronunciation, syllable structure, and how sounds are affected depending on what comes before and after a consonant/vowel.

You might have noticed that there are many rules and exceptions to remember, but it's virtually impossible and meaningless for us to list all of them.

Instead, the best way to learn them is through practice! We'll provide you with numerous examples and practice questions, so buckle up and let's get started!

PRACTICE QUIZ

We've learned that Korean consonants can be used as both initial consonants and final consonants (batchim).
Match the following puzzle pieces to complete a word.

kkum (dream)	chaek (book)	kong (bean)	ot (clothes)	son (hand)	jib (home)	mal (horse)

mom (body)	yong (dragon)	gong (ball)	room (room)	som (cotton)	nun (eye)	bom (spring)

ANSWER : Top row : 꿈 / 책 / 콩 / 옷 / 손 / 집 / 말   Bottom row : 몸 / 용 / 공 / 룸 / 솜 / 눈 / 봄

19

We've learned that certain final consonants (batchim) affect the following consonant. Choose the pronunciation that is correctly transcribed.

1.목과
A.목와 [mok-wa] B. 목꽈 [mok-kkwa]
C. 목화 [mok-hwa] D. 목똬 [mok-ddwa]

2.돈도
A.돈오 [don-o] B. 돈또 [don-ddo]
C. 돈토 [don-to] D. 돈도 [don-do]

3.잇게
A.잇에 [it-e] B. 잇께 [it-kke]
C. 잇쎄 [it-sse] D. 잇쩨 [it-jje]

4.맞아
A.맞싸 [mat-ssa] B. 마자 [ma-ja]
C. 마아 [ma-a] D. 맞사 [mat-sa]

5.꽃이
A.꼬시 [kko-si] B. 꼬지 [kko-ji]
C. 꼬치 [kko-chi] D. 꼬이 [kko-i]

6.놓다
A.노타 [no-ta] B. 노아 [no-a]
C. 노하 [no-ha] D. 노따 [no-dda]

7.울고
A.울꼬 [ul-kko] B. 우꼬 [u-kko]
C. 울코 [ul-ko] D. 울고 [ul-go]

8.밥을
A.밥슬 [bap-sŭl] B. 바블 [ba-bŭl]
C. 바플 [ba-pŭl] D. 바플 [[ba-pŭl]

9.숲과
A.숲와 [sup-wa] B. 숲콰 [sup-kwa]
C. 숲꽈 [sup-kkwa] D. 숲솨 [sup-swa]

10.공을
A.곤글 [gon-gŭl] B. 공를 [gong-rŭl]
C. 고을 [go-ŭl] D. 공을 [gong-ŭl]

11. 방과
A.방꽈 [bang-kkwa] B. 방콰 [bang-kwa]
C. 방과 [bang-gwa] D. 방와 [bang-wa]

ANSWER : 1. B. 목꽈 [mok-kkwa] 2. D. 돈도 [don-do] 3. B. 잇께 [it-kke]
4. B. 마자 [ma-ja] 5. C. 꼬치 [kko-chi] 6. A.노타 [no-ta] 7. D. 울고 [ul-go]
8. B. 바블 [ba-bŭl] 9. C. 숲꽈 [sup-kkwa] 10. D. 공을 [gong-ŭl]
11. C. 방과 [bang-gwa]

As we've learned, final consonants fall into three categories based on their pronunciation — K / T / P. Place the correct consonant into the corresponding bag.

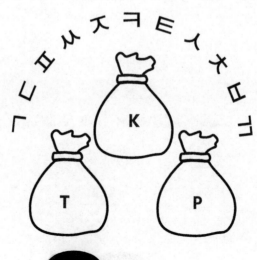

ANSWER :
K : ㄱ ㅋ ㄲ
T : ㄷ ㅌ ㅅ ㅆ ㅈ ㅊ
P : ㅂ ㅍ

We've learned that for double batchim, when followed by a vowel, the first part is pronounced, and the second part goes into the ㅇ. Conversely, when followed by a consonant, only the first part is pronounced, and it affects the following consonant, if applicable. Choose the correct pronunciation.

1. 얇아

A. 얄라 [yal-la] B. 야라 [ya-ra]
C. 얄바 [yal-ba] D. 얍빠 [yap-bba]

2. 앉아

A. 안자 [an-ja] B. 아나 [a-na]
C. 안나 [an-na] D. 안타 [an-ta]

Don't forget the exception rules!

3. 얇게

A. 얄테 [yal-te] B. 얄게 [yal-ge]
C. 얄께 [yal-gge] D. 얍께 [yap-gge]

4. 앉고

A. 앙고 [ang-go] B. 안조 [an-jo]
C. 안코 [an-ko] D. 안꼬 [an-kko]

5. 없다

A. 업따 [ŏp-dda] B. 업사 [ŏp-sa]
C. 업빠 [ŏp-bba] D. 엇다 [ŏt-da]

6. 없이

A. 어비 [ŏ-bi] B. 업씨 [ŏp-ssi]
C. 어이 [ŏ-i] D. 어시 [ŏ-si]

7. 옮다

A. 옴아 [om-a] B. 올따 [ol-dda]
C. 옴따 [om-dda] D. 옴짜 [om-jja]

8. 옮아

A. 오라 [o-ra] B. 올라 [ol-la]
C. 오마 [o-ma] D. 올마 [[ol-ma]

9. 많다

A. 마다 [ma-da] B. 만아 [man-a]
C. 만나 [man-na] D. 만타 [man-ta]

10. 많이

A. 마니 [ma-ni] B. 마히 [ma-hi]
C. 만히 [man-hi] D. 만니 [man-ni]

MP3 〈6〉

CONSONANT #1

기역 (gi-yŏk)

Read out loud as you write!

Initial consonant sound 'g' 가위 [gawi] scissors
Final consonant sound 'k' 수학 [suhak] math

Don't pause! Make it in one stroke!

Try without guide marks!

 MP3 〈7〉

Initial Consonant Sound 'g'	Final Consonant Sound 'k'	Followed by a Vowel	Affecting Following Consonant
고민 [gomin] concern	책 [chaek] book	책아 [chae-ga] [가]	책과 [chaek-kkwa] [꽈]
구름 [gurŭm] cloud	오락 [orak] entertainment	책을 [chae-gŭl] [글]	책도 [chaek-ddo] [또]
개미 [gaemi] ant	이익 [iik] benefit	책우 [chae-gu] [구]	책방 [chaek-bbang] [빵]
가위 [gawi] scissors	기록 [girok] record	책오 [chae-go] [고]	책상 [chaek-ssang] [쌍]
기회 [gihoe] opportunity	직각 [jikgak] right angle	책이 [chae-gi] [기]	책좀 [chaek-jjom] [쫌]
계피 [gyepi] cinnamon	수학 [suhak] mathematics		

CONSONANT #2

니은 (ni-ŭn)

Initial consonant sound 'n' 나비 [nabi] butterfly
Final consonant sound 'n' 기린 [girin] giraffe

Try without guide marks!

 MP3 (8)

Initial Consonant Sound 'n'	Final Consonant Sound 'n'	Followed by a Vowel	Affecting Following Consonant
노인 [noin] old person	돈 [don] money	돈아 [do-na] [나]	
누름 [nurŭm] to push down	오인 [oin] five people	돈을 [do-nŭl] [늘]	
내일 [naeil] tomorrow	이민 [imin] immigration	돈우 [do-nu] [누]	**Does NOT affect following consonant.**
나이 [nai] age	사진 [sajin] photo	돈오 [do-no] [노]	
네모 [nemo] quadrangle	구인 [guin] hiring	돈이 [do-ni] [니]	
뉴욕 [nyuyok] New York	반 [ban] half		

CONSONANT #3

디귿 (di-gŭt)

Initial consonant sound 'd' 다리 [dari] leg
Final consonant sound 't' 숟가락 [sutgarak] spoon

Try without guide marks!

MP3 ⟨9⟩

Initial Consonant Sound 'd'	Final Consonant Sound 't'	Followed by a Vowel	Affecting Following Consonant
도민 [domin] islander	닫다 [dat-dda] to close	닫아 [da-da] [다]	믿고 [mit-kko] [꼬]
다름 [darŭm] difference	믿다 [mit-dda] to believe	닫을 [da-dŭl] [들]	믿다 [mit-dda] [따]
두루미 [durumi] crane	굳다 [gut-dda] to solidify	닫우 [da-du] [두]	믿보 [mit-bbo] [뽀]
더하기 [dŏhagi] addition	듣다 [dŭt-dda] to hear	닫오 [dŭ-do] [도]	믿소 [mit-sso] [쏘]
대화 [daehwa] coversation	쏟다 [ssot-dda] to spill	닫이 [sso-ji] [지] ⚠	믿지 [mit-jji] [찌]
디귿 [di-gŭt] letter ㄷ	_ denotes affected consonant		

24

CONSONANT #4

리을 (ri-ŭl)

Initial consonant sound 'r' 루비 [rubi] ruby
Final consonant sound 'l' 매일 [maeil] everyday

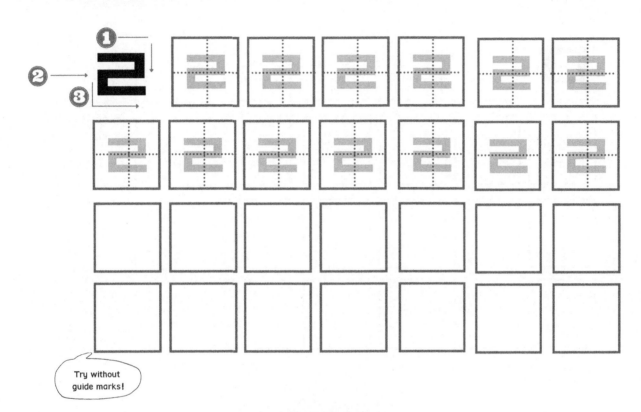

Try without guide marks!

🔊 MP3 (10)

Initial Consonant Sound 'r'	Final Consonant Sound 'l'	Followed by a Vowel	Affecting Following Consonant
라면 [ramyŏn] ramen	돌 [dol] rock	돌아 [do-ra] [라]	
라디오 [radio] radio	발 [bal] foot	돌을 [do-rŭl] [를]	
로마 [roma] rome	오늘 [onŭl] today	돌우 [do-ru] [루]	**Does NOT affect following consonant.**
리어카 [riŏka] handcart	비밀 [bimil] secret	돌오 [do-ro] [로]	
라이터 [raitŏ] lighter	귤 [gyul] tangerine	돌이 [do-ri] [리]	

*Most of the words that begin with ㄹ are foreign words.

25

CONSONANT #5

미음 (mi-ŭm)

Initial consonant sound 'm' 매일 [maeil] everyday
Final consonant sound 'm' 그림 [grim] painting

Try without guide marks!

MP3 〈11〉

Initial Consonant Sound 'm'	Final Consonant Sound 'm'	Followed by a Vowel	Affecting Following Consonant
모자 [moja] hat	모임 [moim] gathering	모임아 [moi-ma] [마]	
무릎 [murŭp] knee	금 [gŭm] gold	모임을 [moi-mŭl] [믈]	
매미 [maemi] cicada	땀 [ddam] sweat	모임우 [moi-mu] [무]	Does NOT affect following consonant.
마을 [maŭl] town	밤 [bam] night	모임오 [moi-mo] [모]	
미국 [miguk] USA	점수 [jŏm-ssu] points/score	모임이 [moi-mi] [미]	
머리 [mŏri] head	＿ denotes affected consonant		

CONSONANT #6

비읍 (bi-ŭp)

Initial consonant sound 'b' 바람 [**b**aram] wind
Final consonant sound 'p' 수입 [sui**p**] import

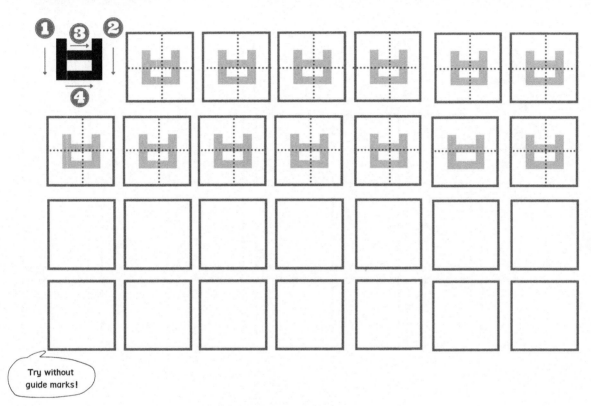

Try without guide marks!

🔊 MP3 〈12〉

Initial Consonant Sound 'b'	Final Consonant Sound 'p'	Followed by a Vowel	Affecting Following Consonant
보기 [**b**ogi] example	집 [ji**p**] home	집아 [ji-**b**a] [**바**]	집고 [ji**p**-<u>kk</u>o] [**꼬**]
부자 [**b**uja] rich person	과즙 [gwajŭ**p**] fruit juice	집을 [ji-**b**ŭl] [**블**]	집다 [ji**p**-<u>dd</u>a] [**따**]
배 [**b**aemi] ship	시합 [shiha**p**] sports (match)	집우 [ji-**b**u] [**부**]	집보 [ji**p**-<u>bb</u>o] [**뽀**]
바위 [**b**awi] rock	수업 [suŏ**p**] (school) class	집오 [ji-**b**o] [**보**]	집소 [ji**p**-<u>ss</u>o] [**쏘**]
비교 [**b**igyo] comparison	입구 [i**p**kku] entrance	집이 [ji-**b**i] [**비**]	집지 [ji**p**-<u>jj</u>i] [**찌**]
버릇 [**b**ŏrŭt] habit			

Refer back to the chart — though the final consonant is pronounced as 'p', it sounds like 'b' when followed by a vowel.

27

CONSONANT #7

시옷 (si-ot)

Sounds somewhere between s and sh

Initial consonant sound 's' 소비 [sobi] to consume
Final consonant sound 't' 비옷 [biot] rain coat

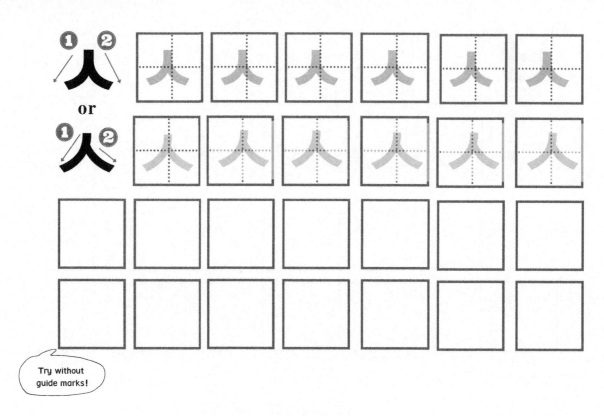

Try without guide marks!

MP3 ⟨13⟩

Initial Consonant Sound 's'	Final Consonant Sound 't'	Followed by a Vowel	Affecting Following Consonant
소주 [soju] soju	옷 [ot] clothes	옷아 [o-sa] [사]	옷고 [ot-kko] [꼬]
수입 [suip] import	빗 [bit] comb	옷을 [o-sŭl] [슬]	옷다 [ot-dda] [따]
새해 [saehae] new year	젓가락 [jŏt-kkarak] chopsticks	옷우 [o-su] [수]	옷보 [ot-bbo] [뽀]
사랑 [sarang] love		옷오 [o-so] [소]	옷소 [ot-sso] [쏘]
시계 [sigye] clock	맛 [mat] taste	옷이 [o-si] [시]	옷지 [ot-jji] [찌]
서류 [sŏryu] documents	넷 [net] four		
	__ denotes affected consonant		

Refer back to the chart — though the final consonant is pronounced as 't', it sounds like 's' when followed by a vowel.

28

CONSONANT #8

이응 (i-ŭng)

Initial consonant sound 'silent' 아기 [agi] baby

*Therefore it's the sound of the vowel.

Final consonant sound 'ng' 봉 [bong] pole

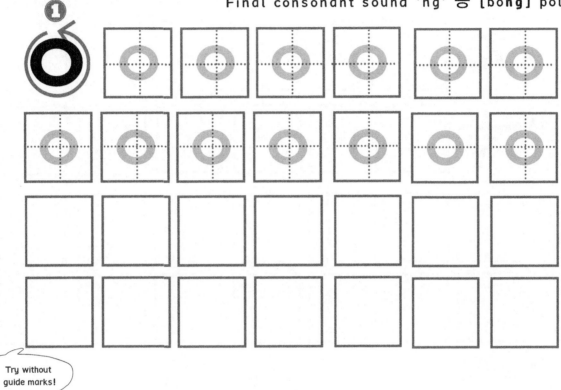

Try without guide marks!

MP3 (14)

Initial Consonant Sound 'silent' (vowel sound)	Final Consonant Sound 'ng'	Followed by a Vowel	Affecting Following Consonant
오빠 [obba] older brother	징 [jing] gong	징아 [jing-a] [아]	
우표 [upyo] postage	등 [dŭng] lamp	징을 [jing-ŭl] [을]	
애인 [aein] lover	지방 [jibang] fat	징우 [jing-u] [우]	**Does NOT affect following consonant.**
아기 [agi] baby	가정 [gaŏng] household	징오 [jing-o] [오]	
이름 [irŭn] name	공부 [gongbu] study	징이 [jing-i] [이]	
어부 [ŏbu] fisherman			

no change

29

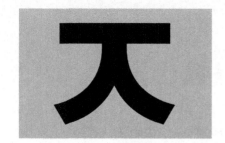

CONSONANT #9

지읒 (ji-ŭt)

Initial consonant sound 'j' 자비 [jabi] mercy
Final consonant sound 't' 낮 [nat] daytime

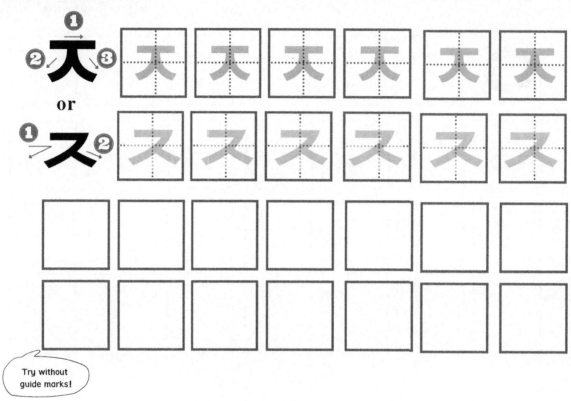

Try without guide marks!

MP3 (15)

Initial Consonant Sound 'j'	Final Consonant Sound 't'	Followed by a Vowel	Affecting Following Consonant
조개 [jogae] clam	젖 [jŏt] milk	젖아 [jŏ-ja] [자]	젖고 [jŏt-<u>kko</u>] [꼬]
주름 [jurŭm] wrinkle	곶 [got] cape	젖을 [jŏ-jŭl] [즐]	젖다 [jŏt-<u>dda</u>] [따]
재미 [jaemi] fun	벚꽃 [bŏtkkot] cherry blossom	젖우 [jŏ-ju] [주]	젖보 [jŏt-<u>bbo</u>] [뽀]
자유 [jayu] freedom		젖오 [jŏ-jo] [조]	젖소 [jŏt-<u>sso</u>] [쏘]
지구 [jigu] earth		젖이 [jŏ-ji] [지]	젖지 [jŏt-<u>jji</u>] [찌]
저울 [jŏul] scale			

Refer back to the chart — though the final consonant is pronounced as 't', it sounds like 'j' when followed by a vowel.

30

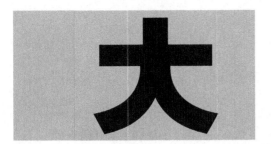

CONSONANT #10

치읏 (chi-ŭt)

Initial consonant sound 'ch' 차비 [chabi] car fare
Final consonant sound 't' 꽃 [kkot] flower

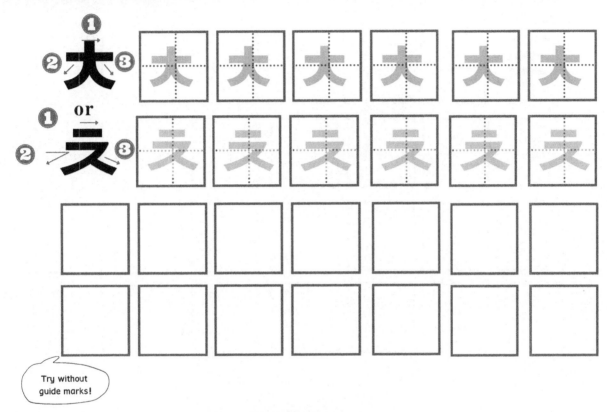

Try without guide marks!

MP3 ⟨16⟩

Initial Consonant Sound 'ch'	Final Consonant Sound 't'	Followed by a Vowel	Affecting Following Consonant
초록 [chorok] green	빛 [bit] light	빛아 [bi-cha] [차]	빛고 [bit-kko] [꼬]
추가 [chuga] addition	낯 [nat] face	빛을 [bi-chŭl] [츨]	빛다 [bit-dda] [따]
채도 [chaedo] chroma	숯 [sut] charcoal	빛우 [bi-chu] [추]	빛보 [bit-bbo] [쁘]
차도 [chado] roadway	돛 [dot] sail	빛오 [bi-cho] [초]	빛소 [bit-sso] [쏘]
치아 [chia] tooth		빛이 [bi-chi] [치]	빛지 [bit-jji] [찌]
처리 [chŏri] to process			

Refer back to the chart — though the final consonant is pronounced as 't', it sounds like 'c' when followed by a vowel.

31

CONSONANT #11

키읔 (ki-ŭk)

Initial consonant sound 'k' 쿠키 [kuki] cookie
Final consonant sound 'k' 부엌[buŏk] kitchen

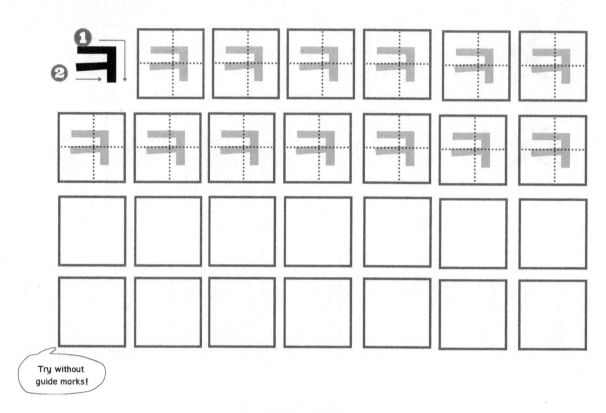

Try without guide marks!

🔊 MP3 〈17〉

Initial Consonant Sound 'k'	Final Consonant Sound 'k'	Followed by a Vowel	Affecting Following Consonant
코골이 [kogori] snoring	부엌 [buŏk] kitchen	부엌아 [buŏ-ka] [카]	부엌고 [buŏk-kko] [꼬]
쿠바 [kuba] Cuba	남녘 [namnyŏk] southern	부엌을 [buŏ-kŭl] [클]	부엌다 [buŏk-dda] [따]
캐나다 [kaenada] Canada		부엌우 [buŏ-ku] [쿠]	부엌보 [buŏk-bbo] [뽀]
카메라 [kamera] camera	Words ending with a ㅋ batchim is very rare.	부엌오 [buŏ-ko] [코]	부엌소 [buŏk-sso] [쏘]
키우다 [kiuda] to grow		부엌이 [buŏ-ki] [키]	부엌지 [buŏk-jji] [찌]
커피 [kŏpi] coffee			

티읕 (ti-ŭt)

Initial consonant sound 't' 토끼 [tokki] rabbit
Final consonant sound 't' 솥 [sot] caldron

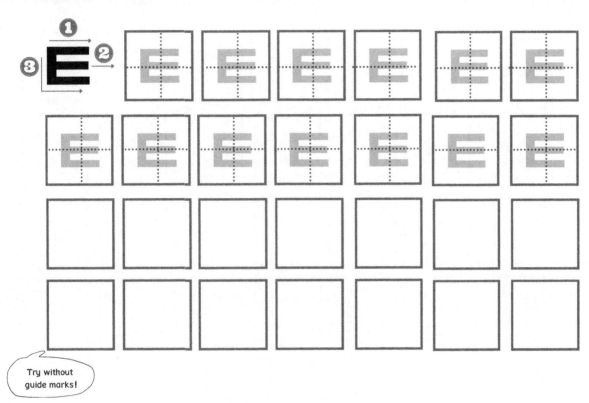

Try without guide marks!

MP3 ⟨18⟩

Initial Consonant Sound 't'	Final Consonant Sound 't'	Followed by a Vowel	Affecting Following Consonant
토기 [togi] earthenware	겉 [gŏt] outside/exterior	겉아 [gŏ-ta] [타]	겉고 [gŏt-<u>kk</u>o] [꼬]
투수 [tusu] (baseball) pitcher	끝 [kkŭt] the end	겉을 [gŏ-tŭl] [틀]	겉다 [gŏt-<u>dd</u>a] [따]
태도 [taedo] attitude	밭 [bat] field/farm	겉우 [gŏ-tu] [투]	겉보 [gŏt-<u>bb</u>o] [뽀]
타조 [tajo] ostrich	팥 [pat] red bean	겉오 [gŏ-to] [토]	겉소 [gŏt-<u>ss</u>o] [쏘]
티끌 [tikkŭl] speck	밑 [mit] bottom/under	겉이 [gŏ-**chi**] [**치**] ⚠️	겉지 [gŏt-<u>jj</u>i] [찌]
터키 [tŏki] Turkey			

33

CONSONANT #13

피읖 (pi-ŭp)

Initial consonant sound 'p' 파도 [**p**ado] wave
Final consonant sound 'p' 풀잎 [puli**p**] grass leaf

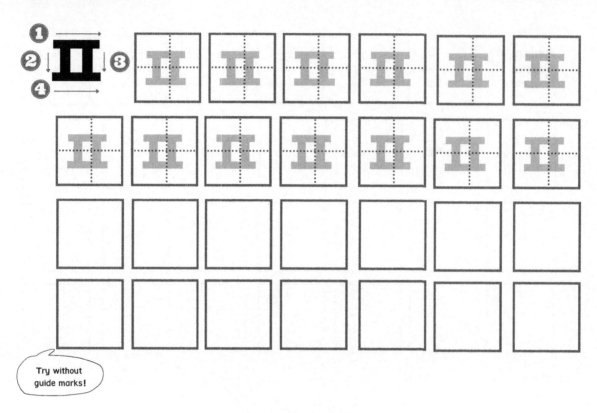

Try without guide marks!

MP3 〈19〉

Initial Consonant Sound 'p'	Final Consonant Sound 'p'	Followed by a Vowel	Affecting Following Consonant
포화 [**p**ohwa] saturation	무릎 [murŭ**p**] knee	잎아 [i-**p**a] [**파**]	잎고 [i**p**-<u>kk</u>o] [**꼬**]
푸름 [**p**urŭm] blueness	앞 [a**p**] front/before	잎을 [i-**p**ŭl] [**플**]	잎다 [i**p**-<u>dd</u>a] [**따**]
패배 [**p**aebae] defeat	헝겊 [hŏnggŏ**p**] piece of cloth	잎우 [i-**p**u] [**푸**]	잎보 [i**p**-<u>bb</u>o] [**뽀**]
파괴 [**p**agoe] destruction	잎 [i**p**] leaf	잎오 [i-**p**o] [**포**]	잎소 [i**p**-<u>ss</u>o] [**쏘**]
피구 [**p**igu] dodgeball		잎이 [i-**p**i] [**피**]	잎지 [i**p**-<u>jj</u>i] [**찌**]
퍼짐 [**p**ŏjim] diffusion			

34

CONSONANT #14

히읗 (hi-ŭt)

Initial consonant sound 'h' 하마 [ɦama] hippo
Final consonant sound 't' 닿다 [dat–dda] to reach

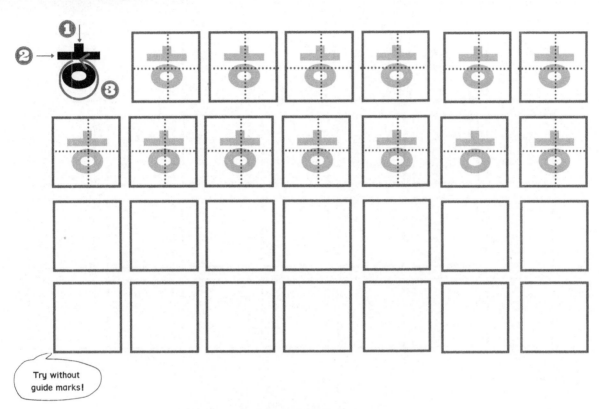

Try without guide marks!

MP3 ⟨20⟩

Initial Consonant Sound 'h'	Final Consonant Sound 't'	Followed by a Vowel	Affecting Following Consonant
호박 [hobak] pumpkin	빻다 [bbat-<u>ta</u>] to grind	닿아 [da-a] [아]	닿고 [dat-<u>kk</u>o] [꼬]
후추 [huchu] black pepper	낳다 [nat-<u>ta</u>] to give birth	닿을 [da-ŭl] [을]	닿다 [dat-<u>dd</u>a] [따]
해안 [haean] coastal line	놓다 [not-<u>ta</u>] to let go	닿우 [da-u] [우]	닿보 [dat-<u>bb</u>o] [뽀]
하늘 [hanŭl] sky	하얗다 [hayat-<u>ta</u>] is white	닿오 [da-o] [오]	닿소 [dat-<u>ss</u>o] [쏘]
히잡 [hijap] hijab	_ denotes affected consonant	닿이 [da-i] [이]	닿지 [dat-<u>jj</u>i] [찌]
허리 [hŏri] waist			

Refer back to the chart — though the final consonant is prounced as 't', it is silent when followed by a vowel (it's the sound of the vowel).

35

CONSONANT #15

쌍기역 (ssang gi-yŏk)

Initial consonant sound 'kk' 꿀 [kkul] honey
Final consonant sound 'k' 깎다 [kkak-dda] to carve

Try without guide marks!

Initial Consonant Sound 'kk'	Final Consonant Sound	Followed by a Vowel	Affecting Following Consonant
꼬마 [**kk**oma] little kid	꺾다 [kkŏ**k**-dda] to snap	꺾어 [kkŏk-**kk**ŏ] [**꺼**]	꺾다 [kkŏk-**dd**a] [**따**]
꾸중 [**kk**ujung] scolding	엮다 [yŏ**k**-dda] to weave	엮어 [yŏk-**kk**ŏ] [**꺼**]	엮다 [yŏk-**dd**a] [**따**]
깨 [**kk**ae] sesame	깎다 [kka**k**-dda] to carve	깎아 [kka-**kk**a] [**까**]	깎다 [kka-**dd**a] [**따**]
까마귀 [**kk**amagwi] crow	낚시 [na**k**-ssi] fishing	낚아 [nak-**kk**a] [**까**]	낚시 [nak-**ss**i] [**씨**]
끼니 [**kk**ini] meal			
꺼내다 [**kk**ŏnaeda] to pull out			

CONSONANT #16

쌍디귿 (ssang di-gŭt)

Initial consonant sound 'h' 하마 [ɦama] hippo
Final consonant sound 't' 닿다 [dat-dda] to reach

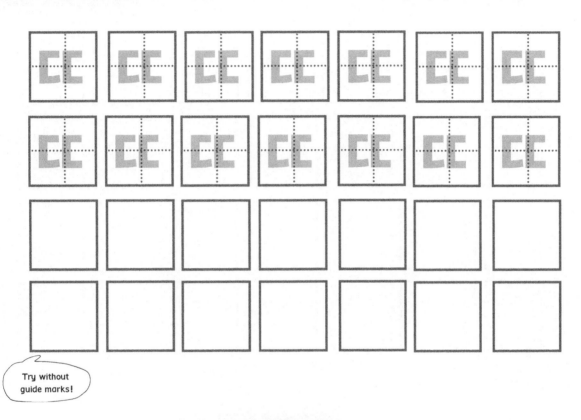

Try without guide marks!

MP3 〈22〉

Initial Consonant Sound 'dd'	Final Consonant Sound	Followed by a Vowel	Affecting Following Consonant
또 [**dd**o] again	Technically, it should be pronounced the same as ㄷ batchim (t), but there are no words in Korean that use ㄸ as batchim.	Technically, it should be pronounced the same as ㄷ batchim (t), but there are no words in Korean that use ㄸ as batchim.	Technically, it should be pronounced the same as ㄷ batchim (t), so it would have affected following consonant the same way ㄷ (t) would.
뚜껑 [**dd**ukkŏng] lid			
때 [**dd**ae] moment			
따귀 [**dd**agwi] slap			
띠 [**tt**i] belt			
떠돌이 [**tt**ŏdori] wanderer			

37

CONSONANT #17

쌍비읍 (ssang bi-ŭp)

Initial consonant sound 'bb' 뿔 [**bb**ul] horn
Final consonant sound NOT APPLICABLE

Try without guide marks!

Initial Consonant Sound 'bb'	Final Consonant Sound	Followed by a Vowel	Affecting Following Consonant
뽀뽀 [**bb**o**bb**o] kiss			
뿌리 [**bb**uri] root	Technically, it should be pronounced the same as ㅂ batchim (p), but there are no words in Korean that use ㅃ as batchim.	Technically, it should be pronounced the same as ㅂ batchim (p), but there are no words in Korean that use ㅃ as batchim.	Technically, it should be pronounced the same as ㅂ batchim (p), so it would have affected following consonant the same way ㅂ (p) would.
빼기 [**bb**aegi] subtraction			
뼈 [**bb**yŏ] bone			

CONSONANT #18

쌍시옷 (ssang si-ot)

Initial consonant sound 'ss' 씨 [ssi] seed
Final consonant sound 't' 있다 [it-dda] exist

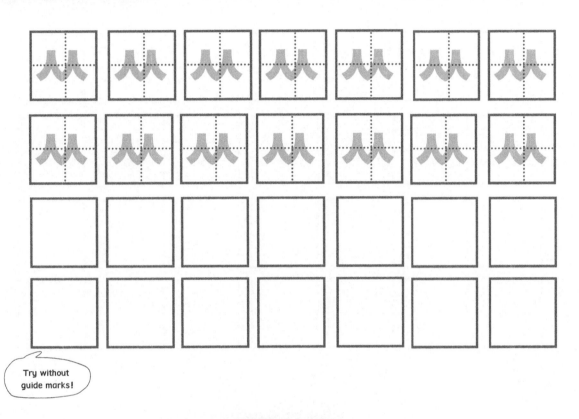

Try without guide marks!

MP3 (24)

Initial Consonant Sound 'ss'	Final Consonant Sound 't'	Followed by a Vowel	Affecting Following Consonant
싹 [ssak] sprout	했다 [haet-dda] (I) did	했아 [hae-ssa] [싸]	했고 [haet-kko] [꼬]
쑥 [ssuk] mugwort	갔다 [gat-dda] (I) went	했을 [hae-ssŭl] [쓸]	했다 [haet-dda] [따]
싸움 [ssaum] fight	봤다 [bwat-dda] (I) saw	했우 [hae-ssu] [쑤]	했보 [haet-bbo] [뽀]
쏘다 [ssoda] to shoot	__ denotes affected consonant	했오 [hae-sso] [쏘]	했소 [haet-sso] [쏘]
씨름 [ssirŭm] Korean wrestling		했이 [hae-ssi] [씨]	했지 [haet-jji] [찌]

Refer back to the chart — though
the final consonant is prounced as
't', it sounds like 'ss' when
followed by a vowel.

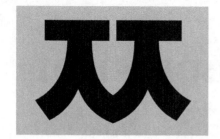

CONSONANT #19

쌍지읓 (ssang ji-ŭt)

Initial consonant sound 'jj' 쪽 [jjok] page
Final consonant sound NOT APPLICABLE

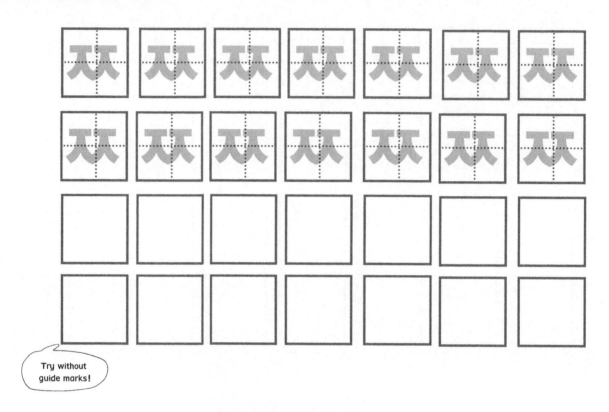

Try without guide marks!

🔊 **MP3 〈25〉**

Initial Consonant Sound 'jj'	Final Consonant Sound	Followed by a Vowel	Affecting Following Consonant
짜장면 [**jj**ajangmyŏn] black noodle			
짬 [**jj**am] time	Technically, it should be pronounced the same as ㅈ batchim (t), but there are no words in Korean that use ㅉ as batchim.	Technically, it should be pronounced the same as ㅈ batchim (t), but there are no words in Korean that use ㅉ as batchim.	Technically, it should be pronounced the same as ㅈ batchim (t), so it would have affected following consonant the same way ㅈ (t) would.
찜 [**jj**im] steaming			
짝 [**jj**ak] pair			
찌개 [**jj**igae] stew			

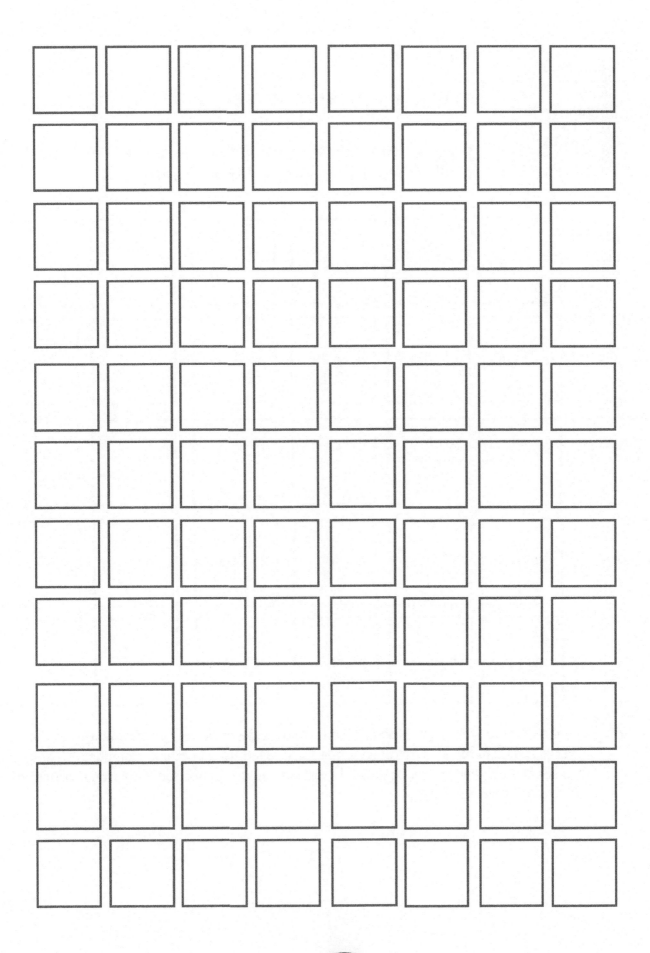

VOWEL #1

TYPE : RIGHT SIDE VOWEL

(a) English Approximation – Papa
Korean Exmaple 자두 [jadu]

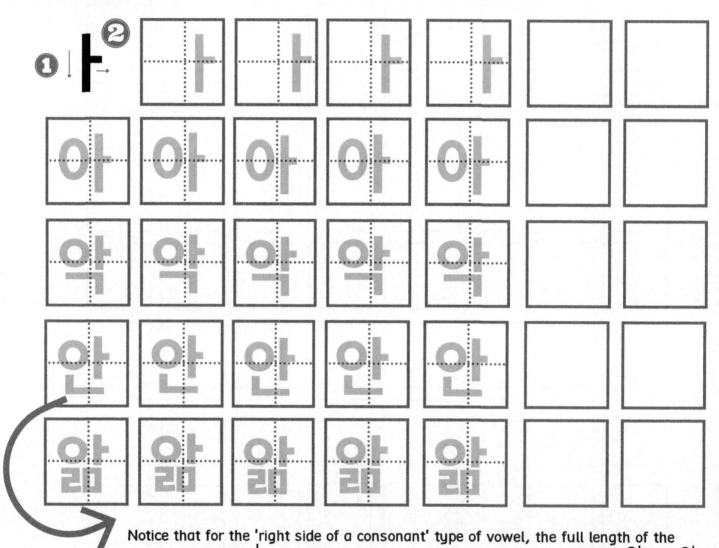

Notice that for the 'right side of a consonant' type of vowel, the full length of the vertical bottom of ㅏ is retained when ㄴ is used as a batchim. Compare 악 and 안 to see the difference. It's because ㄴ provides extra space for the vertical bottom of ㅏ to fully stretch out.

VOWEL #2

TYPE : RIGHT SIDE VOWEL

English Approximation – See **ya**!
Korean Exmaple 야구 [**yagu**] baseball **(ya)**

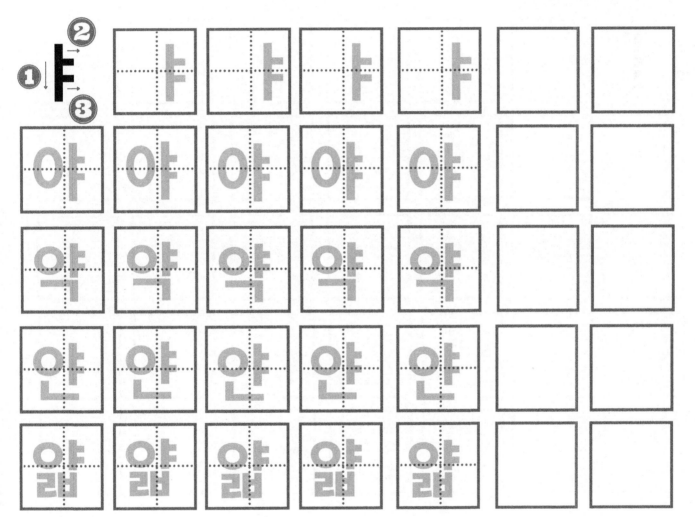

VOWEL #3

TYPE : RIGHT SIDE VOWEL

(ŏ) English Approximation – **u**p
Korean Example 접시 [jŏpsi] dish

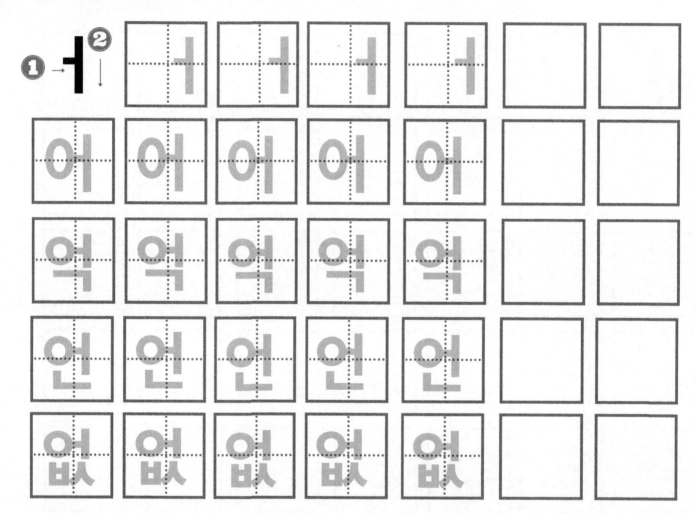

VOWEL #4

TYPE : RIGHT SIDE VOWEL

ㅕ

English Approximation – *young*
Korean Example 영화[yŏnghwa] movie
(yŏ)

ㅕ	ㅕ	ㅕ	ㅕ		
어	어	어	어	어	
역	역	역	역	역	
연	연	연	연	연	
열	열	열	열	열	

VOWEL #5

TYPE : LOWER SIDE VOWEL

(o) English Approximation – *over*
Korean Exmaple 오리 [ori] duck

VOWEL #6

TYPE : LOWER SIDE VOWEL

English Approximation – yogurt
Korean Example 요리 [yori] cooking

(yo)

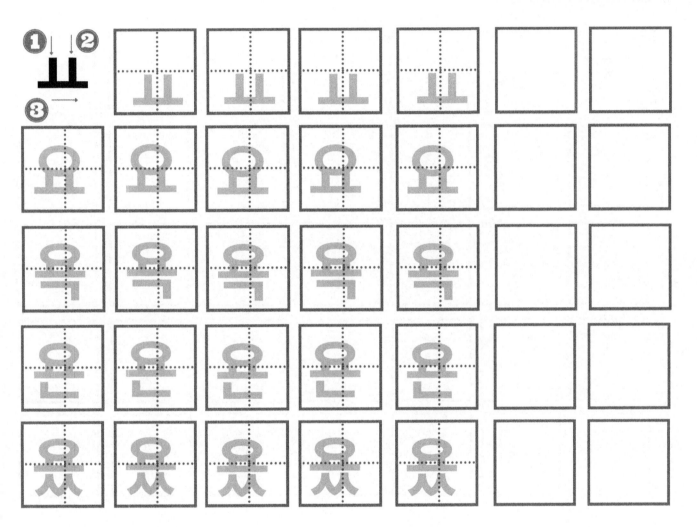

VOWEL #7

TYPE : LOWER SIDE VOWEL

(u) English Approximation — root
Korean Example 자두 [jadu]

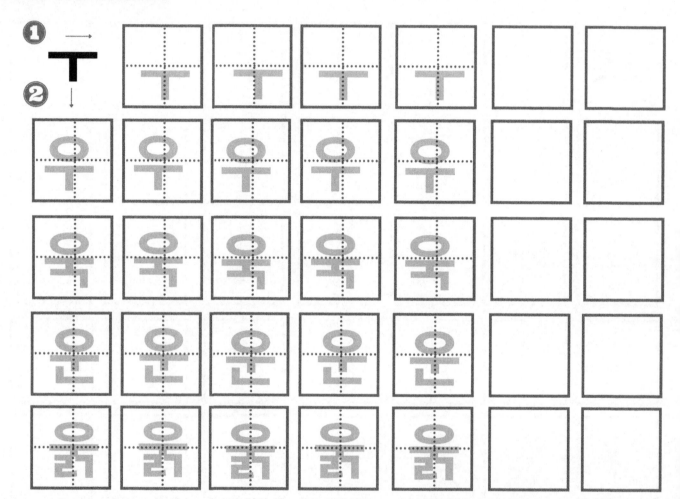

VOWEL #8

TYPE : LOWER SIDE VOWEL

English Approximation – *you*
Korean Example 소유 [so*y*u] possession **(yu)**

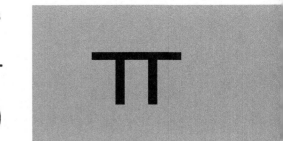

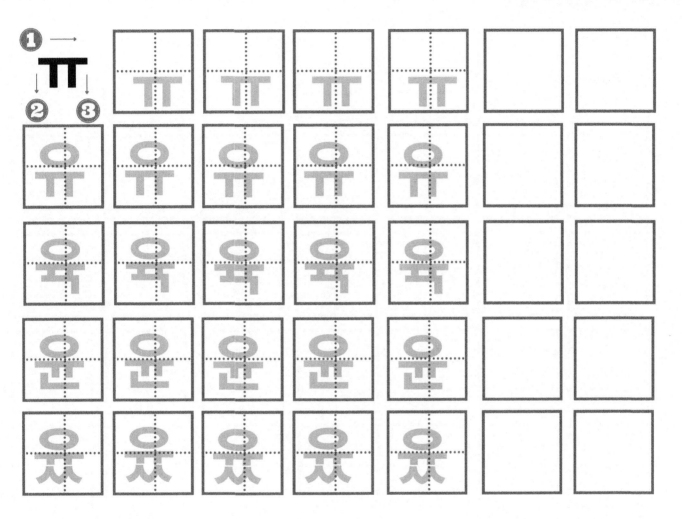

VOWEL #9

TYPE : LOWER SIDE VOWEL

(a) English Approximation – good
Korean Example 그림 [gŭrim] painting

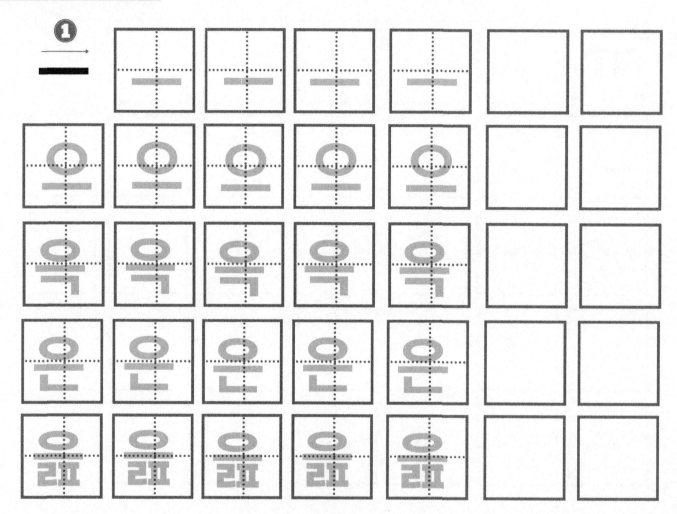

VOWEL #10

TYPE : RIGHT SIDE VOWEL

English Approximation – hit
Korean Example 소리 [sori] sound

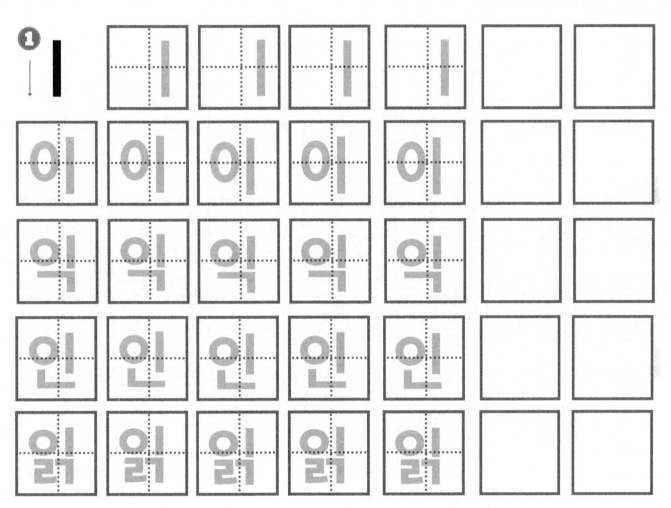

VOWEL #11

TYPE : RIGHT SIDE VOWEL

(e) English Approximation – energy
Korean Example 세기 [segi] strength

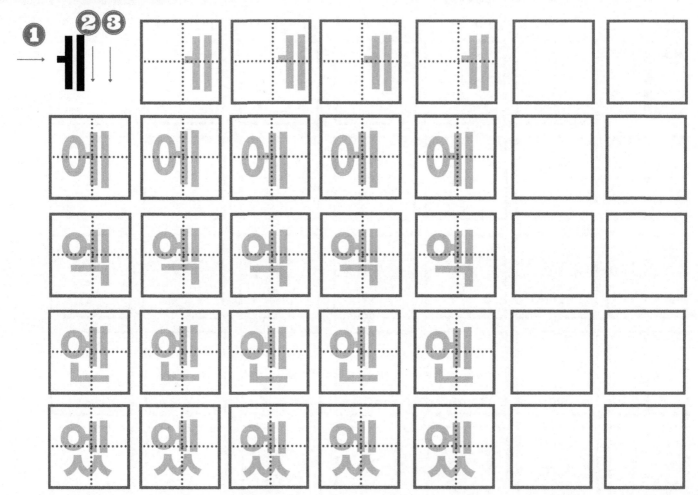

VOWEL #12

TYPE : RIGHT SIDE VOWEL

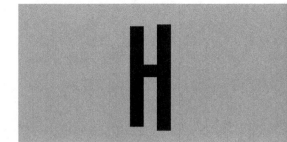

English Approximation – table
Korean Example 애기 [aegi] baby

(ae)

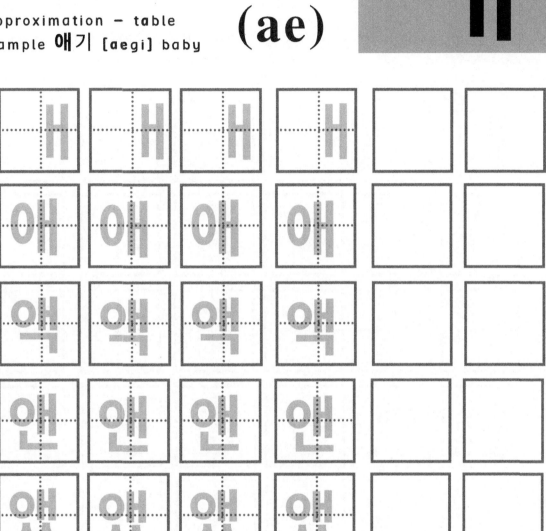

VOWEL #13

TYPE : RIGHT SIDE VOWEL

(ye) English Approximation – yes
Korean Example 예술 [yesul] art

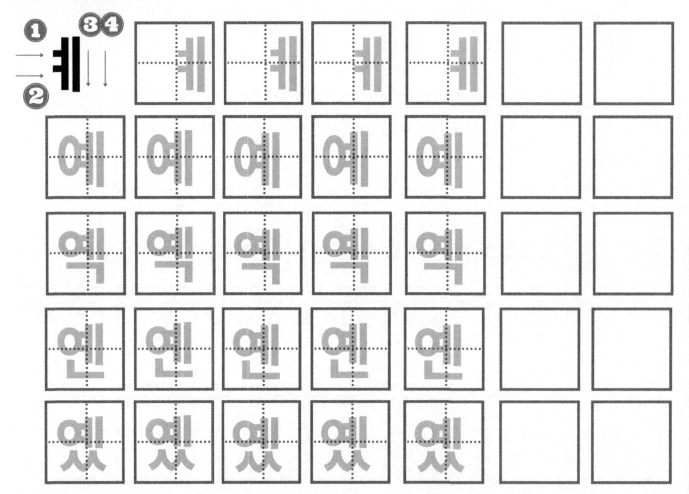

VOWEL #14

TYPE : RIGHT SIDE VOWEL

ㅒ

English Approximation – yes
Korean Example 얘기 [yaegi] story **(yae)**

ㅒ	ㅒ	ㅒ	ㅒ	ㅒ		
얘	얘	얘	얘	얘		
얙	얙	얙	얙	얙		
얜	얜	얜	얜	얜		
얬	얬	얬	얬	얬		

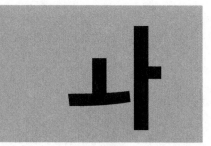

VOWEL #15

TYPE : RIGHT / LOWER COMBINATION VOWEL

(wa) English Approximation – **what**
Korean Example 과일 [gwail] fruit

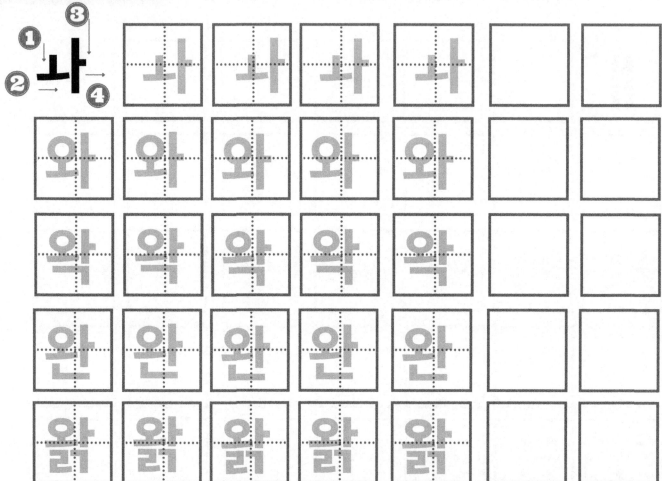

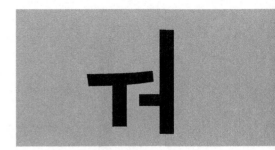

VOWEL #16

TYPE : RIGHT / LOWER COMBINATION VOWEL

English Approximation – wonder
Korean Example 권투 [gwontu] boxing  **(wǒ)**

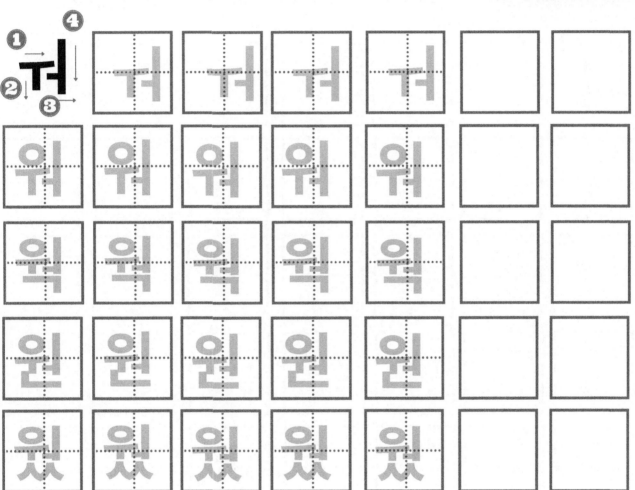

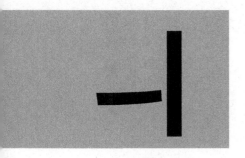

VOWEL #17

TYPE : RIGHT / LOWER COMBINATION VOWEL

(ŭi) English Approximation — We
Korean Example 의자 [ŭija] chair

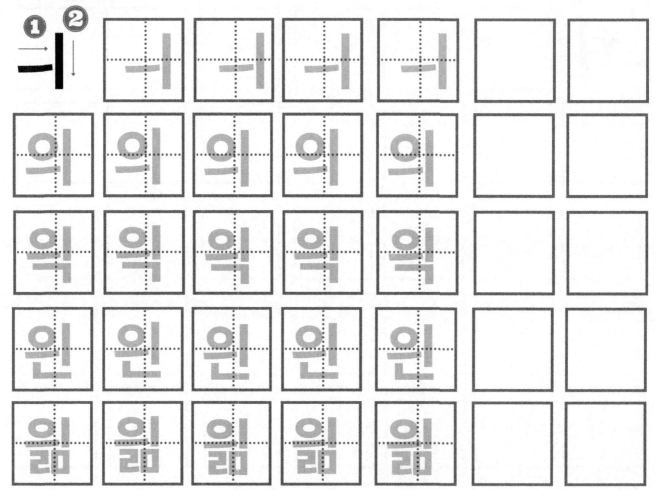

VOWEL #18

TYPE : RIGHT / LOWER COMBINATION VOWEL

English Approximation – wet
Korean Example 최고 [choego] best **(oe)**

While ㅚ is ㅗ + ㅣ so "oi" seems right when followed the rules, it's pronounced as "oe", and it's *not* a "double vowel", either.

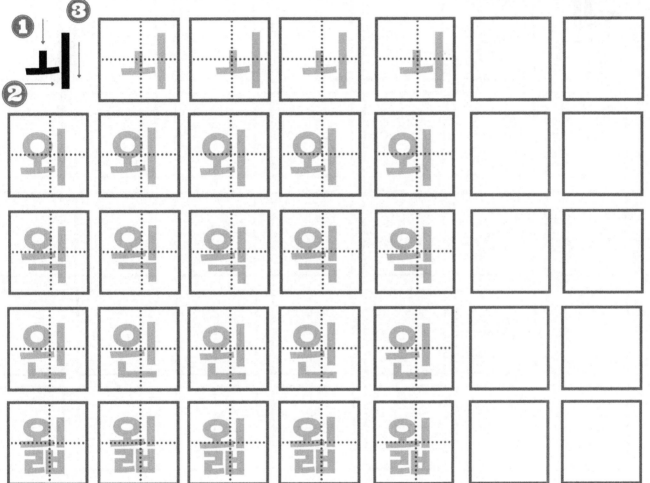

VOWEL #19

TYPE : RIGHT / LOWER COMBINATION VOWEL

(we) English Approximation – quest
Korean Example 훼손 [hweson] damage

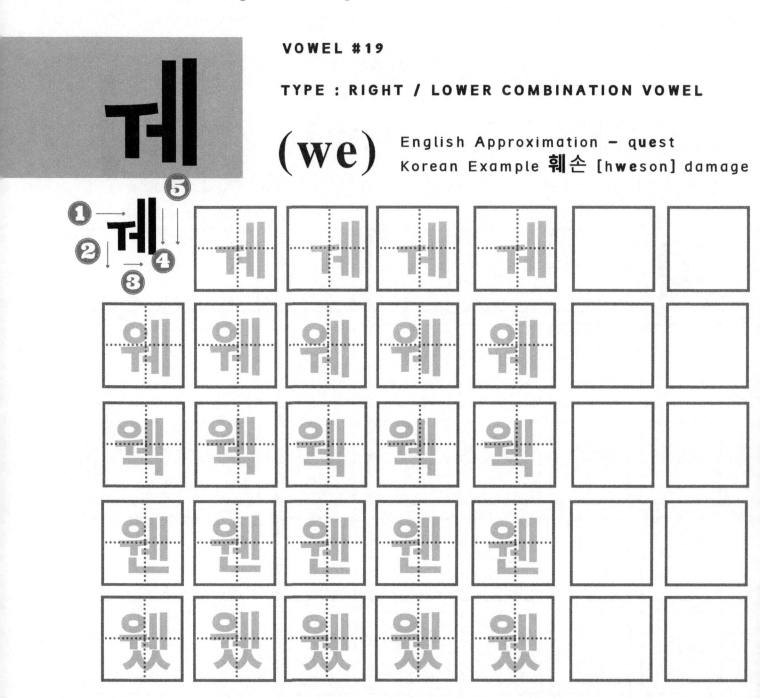

VOWEL #20

TYPE : RIGHT / LOWER COMBINATION VOWEL

English Approximation – where
Korean Example 안돼 [and**wae**] can't

(wae)

SENTENCE STRUCTURE

As you will see, Korean sentences are structured in a different order than English sentences. It might seem strange at the moment, but you will get used to it as we practice more.

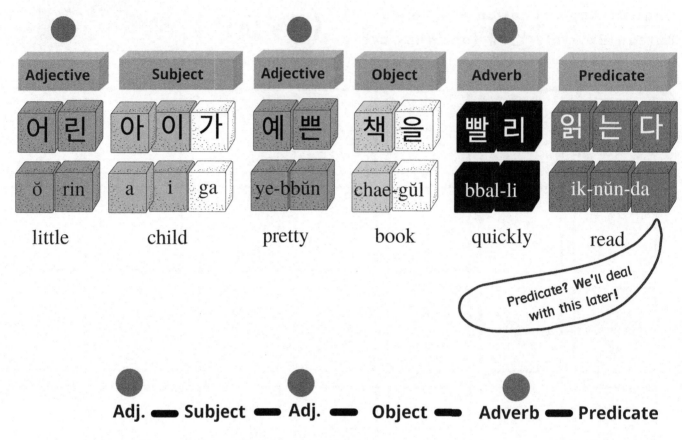

Adjective	Subject	Adjective	Object	Adverb	Predicate
어 린	아 이 가	예 쁜	책 을	빨 리	읽 는 다
ǒ rin	a i ga	ye-bbǔn	chae-gǔl	bbal-li	ik-nǔn-da
little	child	pretty	book	quickly	read

Predicate? We'll deal with this later!

Adj. ● Subject ● Adj. ● Object ● Adverb ● Predicate

The dots indicate that they are not essential to make a sentence have meaning. That is, the subject, object, and predicate are the only necessary elements for a sentence to convey meaning.

아이가 책을 읽는다 = (A) child reads a book.

One thing you should have noticed is 는 that comes right after the subject and 를 which comes immediately after the object. I left them uncolored on purpose! You might have noticed that there is no direct English translation for them. This is because there are no words in English that correspond directly to them. However, they are similar to the concept of "a/the" in English grammar, which cannot be directly translated into Korean. Despite this, you can still understand the meaning of a sentence without them.

So, who are these unsung heroes doing the hard work in the shadows? Let's find out!

WHAT!? 은/는 이/가 을/를

SUBJECT MARKER – 이/가

A subject market comes after the subject to **indicate what/which the subject of the sentence is.** Using the same example,

무엇**이** 높아요? <u>mu-ǒ-**si** no-pa-yo?]</u> <u>What</u> **is** high?

하늘**이** 높아요. [<u>ha-nǔ-r</u>i no-pa-yo] (**It is**) <u>the sky</u>, that is high.

As you can see, 이 is used to indicate what/which the subject is in a given sentence .

• •

누**가** <u>학생</u>인가요? [**nu-ga** <u>hak-saeng</u>-in-ga-y<u>o</u>?] **Who** is a <u>student</u>?

그녀**가** <u>학생</u>입니다. [gǔ-nyǒ-**ga** <u>hak-saeng</u>-ip-ni-da.] (**It is**) her, **who is** a <u>student</u>.

Again, 가 is used when talking about the action/description (who & student) of the subject.

Now, suppose that you answered with a topic marker 는 for the above question, from previous page.

그녀는 학생입니다. [gǔ-nyǒ-nǔn hak-saeng-ip-ni-da.] (As for) her, she is a student.

It simply doesn't make sense, right? The question refers to what/who/which the subject is, but the answer indicates the description of her (i.e., "student").

• •

Which one to use? 가 after a word ending with a vowel (i.e., no batchim), and 이 after a word ending with a final consonant (i.e., 받침).

TOPIC MARKER – 은/는

> In a similar fashion, the main role for a topic marker is to **indicate what's being talked about.** In other words, it focuses on **action/description** of the subject. Although there is no direct translation, you can think of it as "as for".

하늘은 <u>어때요?</u> [Ha-nŭl-**ŭn** <u>ŏ-ddae-yo</u>?] (As for) the sky, **how** is it?

하늘은 <u>높다</u>. [Ha-nŭl-**ŭn** <u>nop-da</u>] (As for) the sky, it's **high**.

As you can see, 은 is used to when talking about action/description (how & high) of the subject .

● ●

그녀는 <u>무엇인가요?</u> [gŭ-nyŏ-nŭn mu-ŏ-sin-ga-<u>yo</u>?] (As for) her, **what** is she?

그녀는 <u>학생입니다</u>. [gŭ-nyŏ-nŭn hak-saeng-ip-ni-da.] (As for) her, she is a **student**.

Again, 는 is used when talking about action/description (who & student) of the subject.

● ●

> Which one to use? 은 after a word ending with a vowel (i.e., no batchim), and 는 after a word ending with a final consonant (i.e., 받침).

PRACTICE QUIZ

Now, identify the SUBJECT and the OBJECT in the following sentences.
Let's use a circle for the subject and a triangle for the object!

EX 강아지가 하늘을 본다.
A puppy is looking at the sky.

귀여운 아이가 차가운 물을 마신다
A cute child drinks cold water.

배고픈 사람이 라면을 먹었다.
A hungry person ate ramen.

늙은 할아버지가 어린 손자를 보았다.
An old grandpa looked at a little grand child.

A quick-witted student like you should have
noticed that what entails a 이/가 is the
subjective and 을/를 is the object!

ANSWER:
Subject 강아지 Object 하늘
Subject 아이 Object 물
Subject 사람 Object 라면
Subject 할아버지 Object 손자

We've learned how sentences are structured in Korean. Let's practice them!
Assemble the following pieces in the correct order to complete a sentence.

마신다	물을	나는
drink	water	I

_____

우리는	영화를	본다	무서운
we	movie	watch	scary

_____

배고픈	급히	고양이가	먹는다	빵을
hungry	hurriedly	cat	eat	bread

_____

천천히	마신다	뜨거운	영희가	차를	예쁜
slowly	drink	hot	Young-hee	tea	pretty

_____

ANSWER: 나는 물을 마신다 / 우리는 무서운 영화를 본다 / 배고픈 고양이가 빵을 급히 먹는다
예쁜 영희가 뜨거운 차를 천천히 마신다

Some of the following words have an incorrect subject/object marker. Circle the ones that are incorrect.

*You do not need to know what the word means because all you need is the skill to accurately identify a word ends with a consonant or a vowel. Let's work on that skill!

사람가	이름이	하늘이
아기이	세모가	
희망이	물가	집가
발가	양이	
미래이	책이	컴퓨터가

ANSWER: 사람가 / 아기이 / 물가 / 집가 / 발가 / 미래이

And we've learned about subject / object markers! Remember when to use 은/는 and 이/가? They depend on whether the word they are connected to ends with a consonant or a vowel. Let's practice them!

Choose between 은/는

엄마 ☐   아빠 ☐   책 ☐   하늘 ☐

*Again, you do not need to know what the word means because what you need to know is whether the word ends with a consonant or a vowel.

콩 ☐   오리 ☐   내일 ☐   잠 ☐

ANSWER: 엄마는 / 아빠는 / 책은 / 하늘은 / 콩은 / 오리는 / 내일은 / 잠은

Choose between 이/가

엄마 ☐   아빠 ☐   책 ☐   하늘 ☐

*You do not need to know what the word means because what you need to know is whether the word ends with a consonant or a vowel.

콩 ☐   오리 ☐   내일 ☐   잠 ☐

ANSWER: 엄마가 / 아빠가 / 책이 / 하늘이 / 콩이 / 오리가 / 내일이 / 잠이

Now that we have learned about the topic/subject markers, let's delve deeper into understanding their subtle nuances! Your grammar doctor, Dr. Kim, is here to assist you!

To be honest, the topic marker and subject marker are elements that native Korean speakers use effortlessly, so when they are asked to explain their functions and meanings, not many can provide a clear answer.

However, for foreigners (excluding Japanese speakers whose language shares similar elements), these markers can be quite confusing to comprehend.

Without further ado, let me explain them to you and provide you with the proper guidance to learn them quickly and easily!
Trust me, I'm a grammar doctor.

"A vs The"

Suppose we're just talking about a new subject, let's say a computer.
In English, we would use the indefinite article 'a' in front of the subject.

After discussing that computer a little more, we would use the definite article "the".
이/가 and 은/는 are similar in this aspect. 이/가 is used when something is mentioned for the first time,
and 은/는 is used to indicate what has been previously mentioned.

 For example,

신발이 크다. [sin-ba-**ri** kŭ-da.] **A** shoe **is** big.
그런데 그 신발은 예쁘다. [gŭ-reon-de **gŭ** sin-ba-**rŭn** ye-bbŭ-da.]
But **the** shoe **is** pretty.

(Notice 그 (the) is added and 은 follows the subject).

Dr. Kim's Prescription

 # "Contrast"

이/가 is used for general statement and 은/는 is used for contrast.

신발이 있다. [sin-ba-**ri** it-dda.] There **is** a shoe.
신발은 있다. 그런데 모자는 없다.
[sin-ba-**rŭn** it-dda. gŭ-reon-de mo-ja-**nŭn** ŏp-dda.]
There *is* a shoe, but there **is** no hat.

Here, 신발 shoe is the main subject of the sentence, and there is no contrast, so it is 이.
In the second sentence, however, a comparison is made between 신발 and 모자.
That's why 은/는 are used in the sentence.

"Emphasis"

For example,

신발이 크기**는** 하다. [sin-ba-ri keu-gi-**nŭn** ha-da.] (The) shoe **is indeed** big.
신발이 예쁘기**는** 하다. [sin-ba-ri ye-bbeu-gi-**nŭn** ha-da.] (The) shoe **is indeed** pretty.

(크기는 and 예쁘기는 are conjugated form of the adjective 크다/예쁘다)

OBJECT MARKER – 을/를

The object marker signifies that a noun is acting as the object in the sentence. As a general rule of thumb, an object in a sentence (a thing or a person) **receives the action and is described by the verb from the subject.**

수지가 <u>책을</u> >읽어요<.

[**su-ji**-ga <u>chae-g**ŭl**</u> >il-gŏ-yo<.] **Suji** >reads< a <u>book</u>.

Here, 수지 is the subject, and 책 is the object, which receives the action from the subject 수지, which is 'read'.

민호가 <u>운동장을</u> >달려요<.

[**min-ho**-ga <u>un-dong-jang-**ŭl**</u> >dal-lyŏ-yo<.] **Minho** >runs< the <u>playground</u>.

Here, 민호 is the subject, and 운동장 is the object, which receives the action from the subject 민호, which is 'run'.

Which one to use? 을 after a word ending with a vowel (i.e., no batchim), and 를 after a word ending with a final consonant (i.e., 받침).

Don't stress yourself over these markers at the moment because Korean people will still be able to understand the meaning of sentences without topic/subject/object markers, though you will sound like a prehistoric man, or an ape from the movie Planet of the Apes.

So my prescription is more practice, and you will get the hang of it before you know it!

69

PREDICATE

In English, only verbs can be predicates, but in Korean, verb and THIS

are both categorized as "predicate". Want to guess what it is?

I might be wrong, but is it... adjective?

You're super brilliant! Can you tell how they differ, then?

That I don't know, teacher!

Well, they are pretty easy! Verb predicates describe —

Verb

movement
action
process
(e.g., run, buy, study)

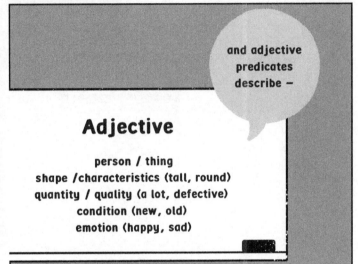

and adjective predicates describe —

Adjective

person / thing
shape / characteristics (tall, round)
quantity / quality (a lot, defective)
condition (new, old)
emotion (happy, sad)

Without them, we can't clearly understand
what the subject does (verb) or what it looks like (adjective), and
that's why adjectives are also called descriptive verbs in Korean!

Korean verbs and adjectives are composed of two parts — a stem and an ending.

먹다 (to eat)

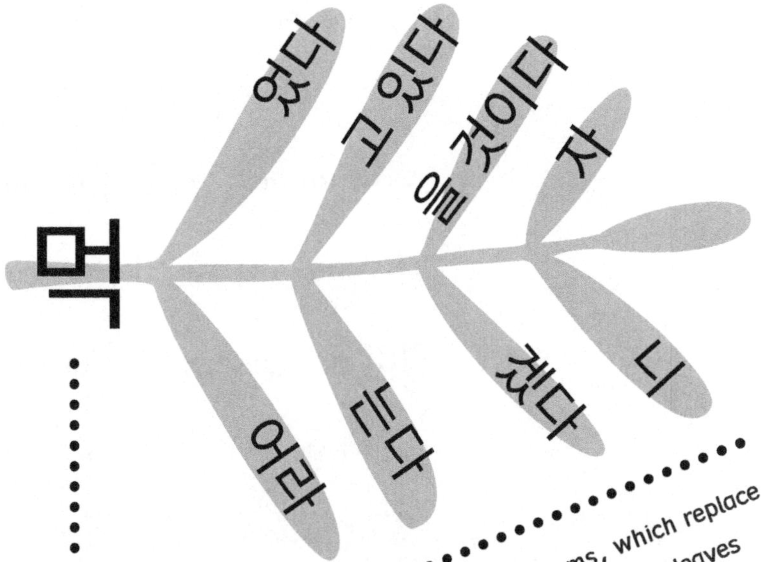

In its base form, a verb or an adjective ends with 다, which is also the form you would use to look up in a dictionary.

먹

었다
고 있다
을 것이다
자
러라
는다
겠다
니

These are conjugated verb forms, which replace the place of 다. These are like the leaves on a stem, because they vary.

What comes before 다 is the stem of a verb.
It's called a stem because it doesn't change.

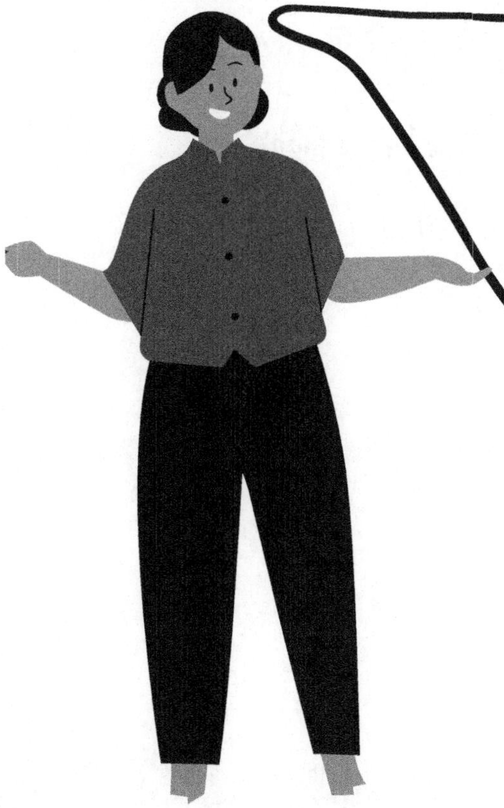

Similarly, an adjective "pretty" is 예쁘다 and "far" is 멀다. Here, the stems for each are 예쁘 and 멀.

Also, ending is conjugated differently depending on the situation (casual, formal, deferential, and etc.) We'll cover this later.

Key point : Both Korean verbs and adjectives can be conjugated.

PRACTICE QUIZ

Let's learn to identify the stem portion of the following predicates!

Underline the stem portion.

먹다 (to eat)   귀엽다 (is cute)   뛰다 (to run)

읽다 (to read)   무섭다 (is scary)   보다 (to see)

입다 (to wear)   느리다 (is slow)   빠르다 (is fast)

구르다 (to roll)   짜다 (is salty)   공부하다 (to study)

멀다 (is far)   길다 (is long)   늦다 (is late)

앉다 (to sit)   배우다 (to learn)   높다 (is high)

ANSWER:
먹 / 귀엽 / 뛰
읽 / 무섭 / 보
입 / 느리 / 빠르
구르 / 짜 / 공부하
멀 / 길 / 늦
앉 / 배우 / 높

Categorize the following set of predicates below

예쁘다 (is pretty)   뛰다 (to run)   느리다 (is slow)

읽다 (to read)   늦다 (is late)   높다 (is high)

아프다 (is sick)   울다 (to cry)   학생이다 (is a student)

1) Person / Thing

2) Movement

3) Shape / Characteristics / Condition

ANSWER:
1) 학생이다 (is a student)
2) 뛰다 (to run) / 읽다 (to read) / 울다 (to cry)
3) 예쁘다(is pretty) / 느리다 (is slow) / 늦다 (is late) / 높다 (is high) / 아프다 (is sick)

Adjectives and Conjugation Rules

> But when an adjective is used as an adjective and not as a predicate, it takes a different form and is always placed BEFORE a noun, with some general rules listed below.

ㄴ

 batchim is added to the adjective stem ending in a vowel.

예쁘다 "is pretty"

As a predicate : 고양이가 **예쁘다**. "The cat **is pretty**."

As an adjective : **예쁜** 고양이 "**pretty** cat"

1) 예쁘 stem remains
2) '다' ending is dropped
3) ㄴ batchim is added to 예쁘, making it 예쁘 + ㄴ = 예쁜

> Remember, it comes before a noun as an adjective!

빠르다 "is fast"

As a predicate : 고양이가 **빠르다**. "The cat **is fast**."

As an adjective : **빠른** 고양이 "**fast** cat"

1) 빠르 stem remains
2) '다' ending is dropped
3) ㄴ batchim is added to 빠르, making it 빠르 + ㄴ = 빠른

은

is added to the adjective stem ending in a consonant.

검다 "is black"

As a predicate : 고양이가 **검다**. "The cat **is black**."

As an adjective : **검은** 고양이 "**black** cat"

1) 검 stem remains
2) '다' ending is dropped
3) 은 is added to 검, making it 검은

> 은 is added here!

얕다 "is shallow"

As a predicate : 호수가 **얕다**. "The lake **is shallow**."

As an adjective : **얕은** 호수 "**shallow** lake"

1) 얕 stem remains
2) '다' ending is dropped
3) 은 is added to 얕, making it 얕은

Irregular ㅂ batchim adjective

ㅂ batchim of the stem is dropped and **운** is added to the stem

---

뜨겁다 "is hot"

As a predicate : 물이 **뜨겁다**. "The water **is hot**."

As an adjective : **뜨거운** 물 "**hot** water"

1) ㅂ batchim of the stem 뜨겁 stem is dropped, leaving 뜨거

2) '다' ending is dropped

3) Instead of '은', '운' is added to 뜨거, making it 뜨거운   **뜨겁다 › 뜨겁은 (x) 뜨거운 (o)**

맵다 "is spicy"

As a predicate : 국이 **맵다**. "The soup **is spicy**."

As an adjective : **매운** 국 "**spicy** soup"

1) ㅂ batchim of the stem 맵 stem is dropped, leaving 매

2) '다' ending is dropped

3) Instead of '은', '운' is added to 매, making it 매운

맵 › 맵은 (x) 매운 (o)

There are many other cases of irregular adjectives and verbs, but knowing the most common types are enough to get you up to speed because you can pick up the outliers as we go along!

Irregular ㅎ batchim adjective

ㄴ batchim replaces the **ㅎ** batchim of the stem

하얗다 "is white"

As a predicate : 눈이 **하얗다**. "The snow **is white**."

As an adjective : **하얀** 눈 "**white** snow"

1) '다' ending is dropped, leaving 하얗 stem

2) ㅎ batchim of the stem 하얗 stem is dropped, leaving 하야

3) Instead of '은', ㄴ batchim goes into where ㅎ was, making it 하얀

하얗다 › 하얗은 (x) 하얀 (o)

동그랗다 "is circular"

As a predicate : 공이 **동그랗다**. "The ball **is circular**."

As an adjective : **동그란** 공 "**circular** ball"

1) '다' ending is dropped, leaving 동그랗 stem

2) ㅎ batchim of the stem 동그랗 stem is dropped, leaving 동그라

3) Instead of '은', ㄴ batchim goes into where ㅎ was, making it 동그란

동그랗다 › 동그랗은 (x) 동그란 (o)

Adjectives and Their Uses

In Korean, adjectives are used to describe the subsequent subject/object more accurately and vividly. Depending on the word you choose, the meaning of a sentence would change drastically.

We just covered how adjectives can be used as predicates similar to verbs.
There are two more possible uses of adjectives.

Describing a Subject

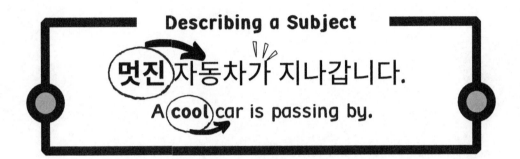

Here, the adjective 멋진 describes the subject 자동차. How do we know which one is a subject and which one is an object? Remember the subject marker 이/가 and the object marker 을/를? 자동차 is followed 가, so it's a subject. Let's look at another example.

Describing an Object

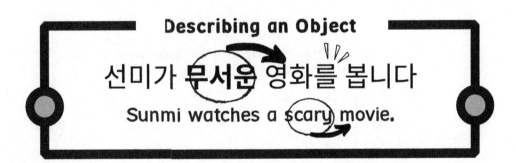

Here, you can see that 무서운 describes the object 영화. We know 영화 is the object (to which an action is performed) here because it's followed by 를, an object marker.

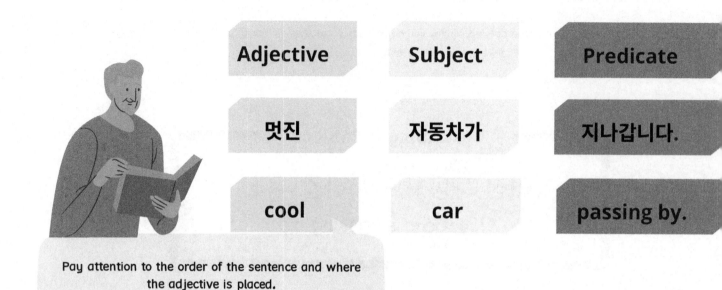

Adjective	Subject	Predicate
멋진	자동차가	지나갑니다.
cool	car	passing by.

Pay attention to the order of the sentence and where the adjective is placed.

A + S + P

Pay attention to the order of the sentence and where the adjective is placed.

A + S + A + O + P

Note that an adjective comes before either a subject or a noun. Very simple!

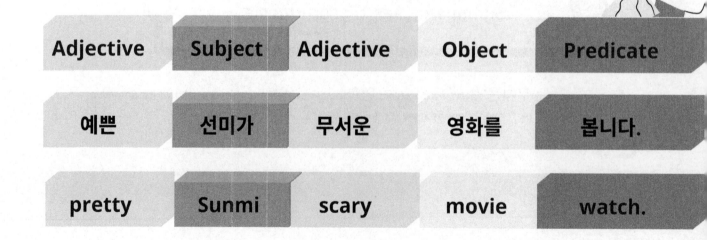

Adjective	Subject	Adjective	Object	Predicate
예쁜	선미가	무서운	영화를	봅니다.
pretty	Sunmi	scary	movie	watch.

PRACTICE QUIZ

Convert the following adjective predicates to base adjective form.

ㄴ batchim is added to the adjective stem ending in a vowel.

무디다 **(is blunt)** > **(blunt)**

못되다 **(is mean)** > **(mean)**

깨끗하다 **(is clean)** > **(clean)**

나쁘다 **(is bad)** > **(bad)**

세다 **(is strong)** > **(strong)**

ANSWER: 무딘 / 못된 / 깨끗한 / 나쁜 / 센

은 is added to the adjective stem ending in a consonant.

얇다 **(is thin)** > **(thin)**

맑다 **(is clear)** > **(clear)**

깊다 **(is deep)** > **(deep)**

낮다 **(is low)** > **(low)**

짧다 **(is short)** > **(short)**

ANSWER: 얇은 / 맑은 / 깊은 / 낮은 / 짧은

ㅂ batchim of the stem is dropped and **운** is added to the stem

가볍다 **(is light)** > **(light)**

쉽다 **(is easy)** > **(easy)**

가깝다 **(is near)** > **(near)**

뜨겁다 **(is hot)** > **(hot)**

싱겁다 **(is bland)** > **(bland)**

ANSWER: 가벼운 / 쉬운 / 가까운 / 뜨거운 / 싱거운

ㄴ batchim replaces the **ㅎ** batchim of the stem

하얗다 **(is white)** > **(white)**

까맣다 **(is black)** > **(black)**

조그맣다 **(is small)** > **(small)**

뿌옇다 **(is cloudy)** > **(cloudy)**

동그랗다 **(is round)** > **(round)**

ANSWER: 하얀 / 까만 / 조그만 / 뿌연 / 동그란

Adverbs

All right! Let's learn about another super important element that's related to the adjectives we just learned. They are adverbs! By definition, adverbs are words or phrases that modify or qualify an adjective, verb, or another adverb or a word group. They express a relation of place, time, circumstance, manner, cause, degree, etc.

For example, in English, the adjective **careful** is **carefully** when used as an adverb.

Adjective

Adverb

quick

quickly

I quickly ran home. = I ran home quickly.

In English, an adverb can be placed before or after a verb, but in Korean, it has to be placed before a verb and can't come before a subject.

s　　adv　　v
나는 집에 빨리 뛰어갔다. (O)

s　adv　　　　v
나는 빨리 집에 뛰어갔다. (O)

s　　　　v　　adv
나는 집에 뛰어갔다 빨리. (X)

adv　s　　　　v
빨리 나는 집에 뛰어갔다. (X)

And there are different types of adverbs, as well as many exceptions to the rules. Therefore, it's easier to familiarize yourself with them, rather than trying to memorize the rules.

Rule #1 하다 -> ~게 / ~히 type

For adjectives ending with "하다", you can either
1) replace the ending 다 with 게, as above, or
2) drop the ending 하다, and replace it with "히"
Both are identical in meaning, but have a subtle difference in nuance.
Native Korean speakers use them interchangeably.

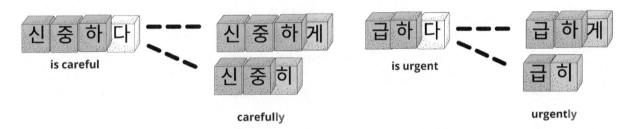

신중하다
is careful

신중하게
신중히
carefully

급하다
is urgent

급하게
급히
urgently

Rule #1-1 하다 -> ~이/히 type

For ~하다 adjectives ending with a batchim ㅅ or ㄱ, either ~이 or ~히 is added to the stem.
It's best to memorize them on a case by case basis.

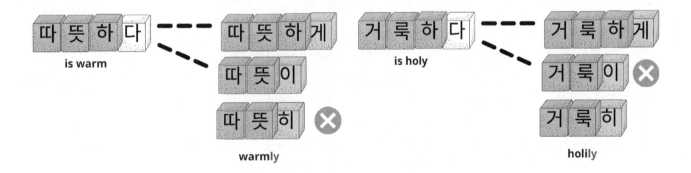

따뜻하다
is warm

따뜻하게
따뜻이
따뜻히 ✕
warmly

거룩하다
is holy

거룩하게
거룩이 ✕
거룩히
holily

Rule #1 Exception Example

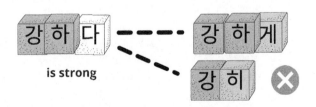

강하다
is strong

강하게
강히 ✕

strongly

Here, 강히 is not an adjective Koreans use, hence this is an example of such exceptions.

So if you see a word ending with ~하게 ~히, you can identify it as an adverb and guess its base form.

Rule #2 ~게 type

For adjectives ending with 다, replace the ending 다 with 게.

아름답**다**
is beautiful

아름답게
beautifully

재밌**다**
is fun

재밌게
funly = (in a fun way)

어렵**다**
is difficult

어렵게
difficultly = (in a difficult way)

PRO TIP When in doubt, it's safe to use ~게, because it works in every situation.

Rule #3 ~적으로 type

And there are adverbs that take the form of a noun + 적으로

기본
basic

기본적으로
basically

열정
passion

열정적으로
passionately

Rule #4 Never Changing Forms

Memorize them and use them in their original form!
Disclaimer : This is NOT an exhaustive list

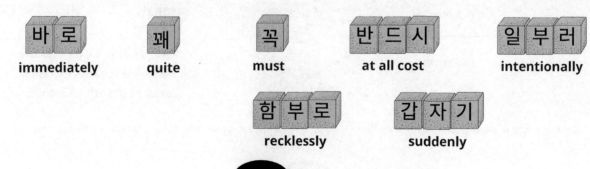

바로
immediately

꽤
quite

꼭
must

반드시
at all cost

일부러
intentionally

함부로
recklessly

갑자기
suddenly

PRACTICE QUIZ

Convert the following adjective predicates to adverb form.

Rule #1 ~하게 / ~히 type

For adjectives ending with "하다", you can either
1) replace the ending 다 with 게, as above, or
2) drop the ending 하다, and replace it with "히"
Both are identical in meaning, but have a subtle difference in nuance.
Native Korean speakers use them interchangeably.

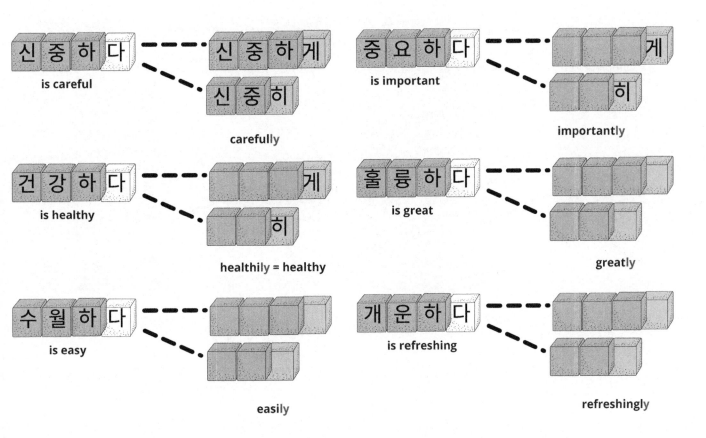

신중하다
is careful

신중하게
신중히
carefully

중요하다
is important

게
히
importantly

건강하다
is healthy

게
히
healthily = healthy

훌륭하다
is great

greatly

수월하다
is easy

easily

개운하다
is refreshing

refreshingly

ANSWER: 중요하게 / 중요히
건강하게 / 건강히　훌륭하게 / 훌륭히
수월하게 / 수월히　개운하게 / 개운히

83

Rule #1–1 ~이/히 type

For ~하다 adjectives ending with a batchim ㅅ or ㄱ, either ~이 or ~히 is added to the stem.
It's best to memorize them on a case by case basis.

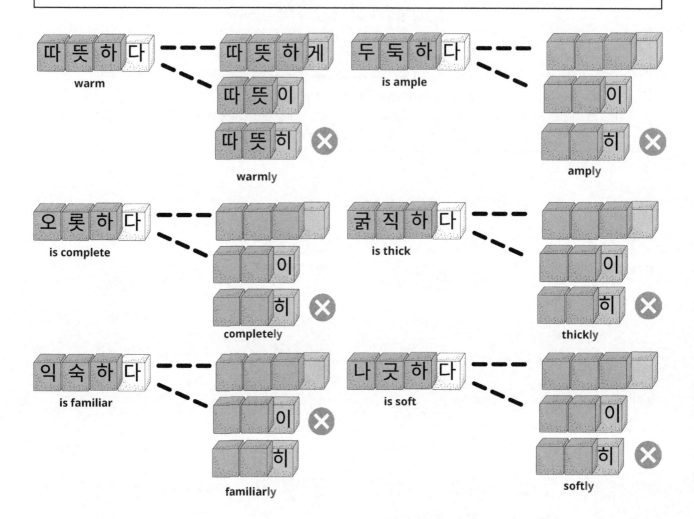

따뜻하다 — warm → 따뜻하게 / 따뜻이 / 따뜻히 ⊗ — warmly

두둑하다 — is ample → 이 / 히 ⊗ — amply

오롯하다 — is complete → 이 / 히 ⊗ — completely

굵직하다 — is thick → 이 / 히 ⊗ — thickly

익숙하다 — is familiar → 이 ⊗ / 히 — familiarly

나긋하다 — is soft → 이 / 히 ⊗ — softly

Pro Tip

When you're not sure what to use 〈이 or 히〉,
then go with ~하게!
You can't go wrong with ~하게!

ANSWER: 두둑하게 / 두둑이
오롯하게 / 오롯이 , 굵직하게 / 굵직이
익숙하게 / 익숙히 , 나긋하게 / 나긋이

Rule #2 ~게 type

For adjectives ending with 다, replace the ending 다 with 게.

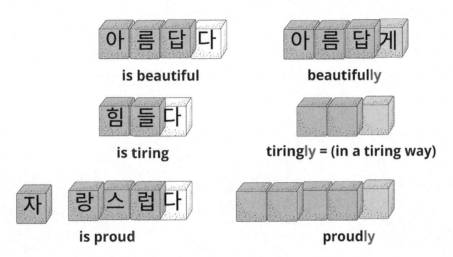

아름답다
is beautiful

아름답게
beautifully

힘들다
is tiring

tiringly = (in a tiring way)

자랑스럽다
is proud

proudly

ANSWER:
힘들게
자랑스럽게

Rule #3 ~적으로 type

And there are adverbs that take the form of a noun + 적으로

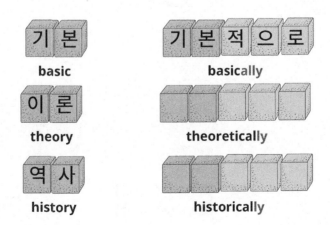

기본
basic

기본적으로
basically

이론
theory

theoretically

역사
history

historically

ANSWER:
이론적으로
역사적으로

IMITATING WORDS

In Korean, there are words that imitate movements and shapes 〈의태어〉 and sounds 〈의성어〉 to make a sentence sound more realistic! Below are some examples. These words are similar in concept and are often used interchangeably because when an action makes a sound, it's about both the action and the sound. No need to split hairs!

콰!

휙!

으르렁!

쿨쿨...

컹컹!

쪽!

철퍽

조잘 조잘

통!통!

As the name suggests, imitating words **describe a movement (action), shape, and sounds, so they come before a predicate (verb or adjective)!** Let's take a look at a few examples.

IMITATING WORD + 하고

IMITATING WORD BY ITSELF

 MP3 〈35〉

대포가 펑! 하고 발사했어요.

A canon went "boom" and launched.

박수를 짝짝짝 쳤어요.

(I) clapped hands, clap clap clap!

물을 꿀꺽꿀꺽 하고 마셔요.

(He) goes "gulp-gulp" and drinks water.

라면을 후루룩 먹어요.

(They) eat ramen slurp-slurp.

Notice how they are used in different ways? The left examples 펑! and 꿀꺽꿀꺽 are followed by 하고, which could be translated as "goes/went" (not literally "to go somewhere").

Conversely, the right examples are used by themselves, without 하고. They are both correct and can be used interchangeably!

INTERCHANGEABLE

MP3 〈36〉

박수를 짝짝짝 하고 쳤어요.

(I) went "clap clap clap" and clapped.

대포가 펑! 발사했어요.

A canon launched. Boom!

라면을 후루룩 하고 먹어요.

(I) went "slurp-slurp" and ate ramen.

물을 꿀꺽꿀꺽 마셔요.

(He) drinks water. Gulp-gulp.

So the above examples, you could have just said 대포가 펑! 발사했어요, without using 하고, to mean "A canon launched, boom!" and 물을 꿀꺽꿀꺽 마셔요, or, the other way around by adding 하고. Easy, right?

PRACTICE QUIZ

Pick the most appropriate imitating word to fill in the blanks.

콩!

휙!

으르렁!

쿨쿨...

컹컹!

쪽!

철퍽

조잘 조잘

통!통!

농구공이 _____ 튀었어요.

A basketball bounced _____.

OR

농구공이 _____ 하고 튀었어요.

A basketball went _____ and bounced.

<u>Remember — there are two ways to use an imitating word.</u>

제트기가 _____ 하고 사라졌어요.

A jet went _____ and disappeared.

OR

제트기가 _____ 사라졌어요.

A jet disappeared. _____!

____! 폭탄이 터졌어요!

A bomb exploded. _____!

OR

_____! 하고 폭탄이 터졌어요!

A bomb went _____ and exploded.

호랑이가 _____ 하고 소리내었어요.

A tiger went _____ and made a sound.

OR

호랑이가 _____ 소리내었어요.

A tiger made a sound. _____.

강아지가 _____ 하고 짖었어요.

A puppy went _____ and barked.

OR

강아지가 짖었어요. _____!

A puppy barked. _____!

어린이들이 _____ 떠들었어요.

Children chatted _____.

OR

어린이들이 _____ 하고 떠들었어요.

Children went _____ and chatted.

소녀가 _____ 하고 뽀뽀했어요.

A girl went _____ and kissed.

OR

소녀가 _____ 뽀뽀했어요.

A girl kissed. _____!

샌드위치가 _____ 하고 바닥에 떨어졌어요.

A sandwich went _____ and fell to the ground.

OR

샌드위치가 _____ 바닥에 떨어졌어요.

A sandwich fell to the ground. _____!

ANSWER: 통!통! / 휙! / 쾅! / 으르렁! / 컹컹! / 조잘 조잘 / 쪽! / 철퍽

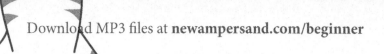

Korean Verbs & Conjugation

Meow! Congratulations on making it this far!

So far, we've learned how to read, write, and pronounce Hangul, and developed an understanding of Korean sentence structure, including topic/subject/object markers, as well as predicates (verbs and adjectives)! With that, you've laid the foundation of the Korean language, and we can build a beautiful house upon it.

One of the most important elements of any language is verbs and their conjugation rules (keep in mind that adjectives can also be conjugated as verbs, and the same rules apply, so there's no need for a separate chapter for the same rules!).

These are some of the characteristics of Korean verb conjugation rules:

- **The basic, unconjugated form ends in 다**

For example, 먹다 (to eat) / 달리다 (to run) / 자다 (to sleep) / 읽다 (to read) they all end in 다.

Korean verbs (and adjectives for that matter, as learned previously) are easy to spot!

Building upon this concept is that

- **To conjugate a Korean verb, the first step is to separate the verb stem from the 다 ending.**

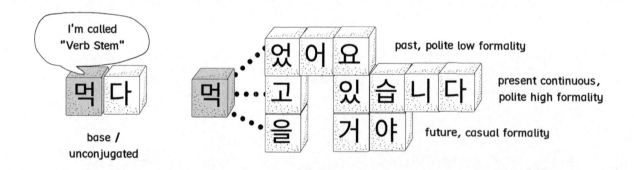

*Don't worry about past/present and polite/casual formality thing for now. We'll cover them later.

- **Unlike English, you don't have to worry about the subject of the sentence when conjugating verbs!**

For example, we say 'I sleep" and "she sleeps", but in Korean, the verb stays the same across all subjects! Seriously, how cool is that?

나는 달린다 – I run 그녀는 달린다 – She runs I It's 달린다 for both 나 I and 그녀 she in Korean.

Another unique aspect of Korean is formality, because there are different conjugation rules depending on who you talk to.

Yo!

'Sup?

Casual Formality

- From someone older to younger (e.g., parents to children)

- Between friends, siblings, people of same age (after building intimacy)

Yes, teacher!

Do your homework!

Polite Low formality

- People you're unacquainted with
- From someone to younger with respect (kindergarten/high school teacher to students)

It's a great pleasure to meet you!

Likewise, ma'am!

Polite High formality

- Official documents
- Between adults (e.g., professor and college student)
- Public service announcement

Let's look at **7** most common tenses used in Korean and their examples!

- Present / Past / Future / Inquisitive Present / Inquisitive Past / Inquisitive Future / Propositive

However, there are more ways of expression (with subtle differences in nuance) than those listed above. But studying the most common ones listed above will give you a solid understanding of the rules!

Present

- Drop the 다 ending from the verb stem
- Add 아요 if the verb ends in a vowel ㅏ or ㅗ. 놀다 (to play) → 놀아요
- Add 어요 if the last vowel of the verb is anything else. 얼다 (to freeze) → 얼어요
- Following the rules above, If the verb stem ends in a vowel, the 아 or 어 that you add to the verb stem will combine with the previous syllable. 보다 (to see) -> 보아요 -> 봐요 (*보 is the verb stem)
- The rules above determine whether 아 or 어 is used in the casual form or 아요 or 어요 is used in the polite form.

Casual formality

Verb (ending in ㅏ / ㅗ) + 아

Verb (ending in anything else) + 어

Polite low formality

Verb (ending in ㅏ / ㅗ) + 아요

Verb (ending in anything else) + 어요

Polite high formality

Verb (ending in a vowel) + ㅂ니다

Verb (ending in a consonant) + 습니다

가다 — to go

Casual formality: 가

Polite low formality: 가요

Polite high formality: 갑니다 (가+ㅂ니다)

읽다 — to read

Casual formality: 읽어

Polite low formality: 읽어요

Polite high formality: 읽습니다

보다 — to see

Casual formality: 봐 (보+아)

Polite low formality: 봐요 (보+아)

Polite high formality: 봅니다 (보+ㅂ니다)

말리다 — to dry

Casual formality: 말려 (말리+어)

Polite low formality: 말려요 (말리+어요)

Polite high formality: 말립니다 (말리+ㅂ니다)

Instead of 하 and 하요, 하다 verb conjugates a little differently, into 해 and 해요. It's one of the most frequently used verbs in Korean, so get used to this!

Also, unlike other verbs, 하다 verb is always combined with a noun to make it a verb. For example, 공부하다 = "doing studying", 노래하다 "doing singing".

하다 — to do

Casual formality: 해

Polite low formality: 해요

Polite high formality: 합니다 (하+ㅂ니다)

92

PRACTICE QUIZ

Identify which of the three formality levels the following present form verbs belong to.

Casual Formality / Polite Low Formality / Polite High Formality

돌다 to turn

돌아요
돕니다
돌아

오다 to come

와
와요
옵니다

노래하다 to sing

노래합니다
노래해
노래해요

긁다 to scratch

긁어요
긁습니다
긁어

ANSWER: 돌다 –> 돌아요 – Polite Low 돕니다 – Polite High 돌아 – Casual
오다 –> 와 – Casual 와요 – Polite Low 옵니다 – Polite High
노래하다 –> 노래합니다 – Polite High 노래해 – Casual 노래해요 – Polite Low
긁다 –> 긁어요 – Polite Low 긁습니다 – Polite High 긁어 – Casual

Convert the following base form verbs into the three formality forms (present).

사다 — to buy
Casual formality:
_____
Polite low formality:
_____
Polite high formality:
_____

입다 — to wear
Casual formality:
_____
Polite low formality:
_____
Polite high formality:
_____

먹다 — to eat
Casual formality:
_____
Polite low formality:
_____
Polite high formality:
_____

ANSWER: 사다 –> 사 / 사요 / 삽니다
입다 –> 입어 / 입어요 / 입습니다
먹다 –> 먹어 / 먹어요 / 먹습니다

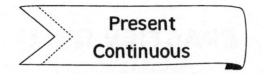

Present Continuous

- Drop the 다 ending from the verb stem and add the following, which means "~ing" in English.

Casual formality	**Polite low formality**
Verb + 고 있어	Verb + 고 있어요

Polite high formality
Verb + 고 있습니다

가다 — **to go**
Casual formality: 가고 있어
Polite low formality: 가고 있어요
Polite high formality: 가고 있습니다

읽다 — **to read**
Casual formality: 읽고 있어
Polite low formality: 읽고 있어요
Polite high formality: 읽고 있습니다

보다 — **to see**
Casual formality: 보고 있어
Polite low formality: 보고 있어요
Polite high formality: 보고 있습니다

말리다 — **to dry**
Casual formality: 말리고 있어
Polite low formality: 말리고 있어요
Polite high formality: 말리고 있습니다

하다 — **to do**
Casual formality: 하고 있어
Polite low formality: 하고 있어요
Polite high formality: 하고 있습니다

PRACTICE QUIZ

Identify which of the three formality levels the following present continuous form verbs belong to.

Casual Formality / Polite Low Formality / Polite High Formality

돌다 to turn

돌고 있어요
돌고 있습니다
돌고 있어

오다 to come

오고 있어
오고 있습니다
오고 있어요

노래하다 to sing

노래하고 있습니다
노래하고 있어요
노래하고 있어

긁다 to scratch

긁고 있습니다
긁고 있어
긁고 있어요

ANSWER: 돌다 –> 돌고 있어요 – Polite Low 돌고 있습니다 Polite High 돌고 있어 Casual
오다 –> 오고 있어 – Casual 오고 있습니다 Polite High 오고 있어요 Polite Low
노래하다 –> 노래하고 있습니다 Polite High 노래하고 있어요 Polite Low 노래하고 있어 Casual
긁다 –> 긁고 있습니다 Polite High 긁고 있어 Casual 긁고 있어요 Polite Low

Convert the following base form verbs into the three formality forms (present continuous).

사다 — to buy
Casual formality:

_____

Polite low formality:

_____

Polite high formality:

_____

입다 — to wear
Casual formality:

_____

Polite low formality:

_____

Polite high formality:

_____

먹다 — to eat
Casual formality:

_____

Polite low formality:

_____

Polite high formality:

_____

ANSWER: 사다 –> 사고 있어 / 사고 있어요 / 사고 있습니다
입다 –> 입고 있어 / 입고 있어요 / 입고 있습니다
먹다 –> 먹고 있어 / 먹고 있어요 / 먹고 있습니다

Past

- Drop the 다 ending from the verb stem
- Add 았다 to the verb stem if the verb ends in either ㅗ or ㅏ. 보다 (to see) –> 보았다.
- Add 었다 if the verb doesn't end in a vowel that's neither ㅗ nor ㅏ. 먹다 (to eat) –> 먹었다.
- Some verbs that end in a vowel will merge. 사다 (to buy) –> 샀다 (o) 사았다 (x)

Casual formality
Verb (ending in ㅏ / ㅗ) + 았어
Verb (ending in anything else) + 었어

Polite low formality
Verb (ending in ㅏ / ㅗ) + 았어요
Verb (ending in anything else) + 었어요

Polite high formality
Verb (ending in a vowel + 았습니다
Verb (ending in a consonant) + 었습니다

가다 — to go
Casual formality: 갔어
Polite low formality: 갔어요
Polite high formality: 갔습니다

읽다 — to read
Casual formality: 읽었어
Polite low formality: 읽었어요
Polite high formality: 읽었습니다

보다 — to see
Casual formality: 봤어 (보+았어)
Polite low formality: 봤어요 (보+았어요)
Polite high formality: 봤습니다 (보+았습니다)

말리다 — to dry
Casual: 말렸어 (말리+었어)
Polite low formality: 말렸어요 (말리+었어요)
Polite high formality: 말렸습니다 (말리+었습니다)

하다 — to do
Casual formality: 했어
Polite low formality: 했어요
Polite high formality: 했습니다

I have a dark past.

96

PRACTICE QUIZ

Identify which of the three formality levels the following past form verbs belong to.

Casual Formality / Polite Low Formality / Polite High Formality

돌다 to turn

돌았어
돌았어요
돌았습니다

오다 to come

왔어요
왔습니다
왔어

노래하다 to sing

노래했어
노래했어요
노래했습니다

긁다 to scratch

긁었어
긁었습니다
긁었어요

ANSWER: 돌다 –> 돌았어 Casual 돌았어요 Polite Casual 돌았습니다 Polite Formal
오다 –> 왔어요 Polite Casual 왔습니다 Polite High 왔어 Casual
노래하다 –> 노래했어 Polite Low 노래했어요 Polite Low 노래했습니다 Polite High
긁다 –> 긁었어 Casual 긁었습니다 Polite High 긁었어요 Polite Low

Convert the following base form verbs into the three formality forms (past).

사다 — to buy
Casual formality:

_____

Polite low formality:

_____

Polite high formality:

_____

입다 — to wear
Casual formality:

_____

Polite low formality:

_____

Polite high formality:

_____

먹다 — to eat
Casual formality:

_____

Polite low formality:

_____

Polite high formality:

_____

ANSWER: 사다 –> 샀어 / 샀어요 / 샀습니다
입다 –> 입었어 / 입었어요 / 입었습니다
먹다 –> 먹었어 / 먹었어요 / 먹었습니다

Future

- Drop the 다 ending from the verb stem
- If the verb ends in a vowel or 을, add ㄹ to the verb stem
- You don't need to add anything to verbs ending in ㄹ, though

---

Casual formality

Verb (ending in ㅏ / ㅗ) + ㄹ 거야

Verb (ending in anything else) + 을 거야

Polite low formality

Verb (ending in ㅏ / ㅗ) + ㄹ 거예요

Verb (ending in anything else) + 을 거예요

Polite high formality

Verb (ending in a vowel) + ㄹ 겁니다 or

Verb ending in a consonant) + 을 겁니다

가다 — to go
Casual formality: 갈 거야
Polite low formality: 갈 거예요
Polite high formality: 갈 겁니다

읽다 — to read
Casual formality: 읽을 거야
Polite low formality: 읽을 거예요
Polite high formality: 읽을 겁니다

보다 — to see
Casual formality: 볼 거야
Polite low formality: 볼 거예요
Polite high formality: 볼 겁니다

말리다 — to dry
Casual formality: 말릴 거야
Polite low formality: 말릴 거예요
Polite high formality: 말릴 겁니다

I'm from the future

하다 — to do
Casual formality: 할 거야
Polite low formality: 할 거예요
Polite high formality: 할 겁니다

This time 하다 follows the rule!

PRACTICE QUIZ

Identify which of the three formality levels the following future form verbs belong to.

Casual Formality / Polite Low Formality / Polite High Formality

돌다 to turn

돌 겁니다
돌 거예요
돌 거야

오다 to come

올 거야
올 겁니다
올 거예요

노래하다 to sing

노래할 거예요
노래할 겁니다
노래할 거야

긁다 to scratch

긁을 거야
긁을 겁니다
긁을 거예요

ANSWER: 돌다 –> 돌 겁니다 Polite High 돌 거예요 Polite Low 돌 거야 Casual
오다 –> 올 거야 Casual 올 겁니다 Polite High 올 거예요 Polite Low
노래하다 –> 노래할 거예요 Polite Low 노래할 겁니다 Polite High 노래할 거야 Casual
긁다 –> 긁을 거야 Casual 긁을 겁니다 Polite High 긁을 거예요 Polite Low

Convert the following base form verbs into the three formality forms (future).

사다 — to buy
Casual formality:

Polite low formality:

Polite high formality:

입다 — to wear
Casual formality:

Polite low formality:

Polite high formality:

먹다 — to eat
Casual formality:

Polite low formality:

Polite high formality:

ANSWER: 사다 –> 살 거야 / 살 거예요 / 살 겁니다
입다 –> 입을 거야 / 입을 거예요 / 입을 겁니다
먹다 –> 먹을 거야 / 먹을 거예요 / 먹을 겁니다

Inquisitive Present

- Drop the 다 ending from the verb stem
- The final vowel determines whether 아 or 어 is used in the casual form or 아요 or 어요 is used in the polite form.
- Use 아요 if the last vowel in the verb is ㅏ or ㅗ. 놀다 (to play) → 놀아요
- Use 어요 if the last vowel in the verb is anything else. 얼다 (to freeze) → 얼어요
- If the verb stem ends in a vowel, the 아 / 어 that you add to the verb stem will combine with the previous syllable.

Casual formality

Verb (ending in ㅏ/ㅗ) + 아?

Verb (ending anything else) + 어?

Polite low formality

Verb (ending in ㅏ/ㅗ) + 아요?

Verb (ending anything else) + 어요?

Polite high formality

Verb Verb (ending in a vowel) + ㅂ니까?

Verb (ending in a consonant) + 습니까?

가다 — to go
Casual formality: 가?
Polite low formality: 가요?
Polite high formality: 갑니까? (가+ㅂ니까?)

읽다 — to read
Casual formality: 읽어?
Polite low formality: 읽어요?
Polite high formality: 읽습니까? (읽+습니까?)

보다 — to see
Casual formality: 봐 (보+아)?
Polite low formality: 봐요 (보+아)?
Polite high formality: 봅니까 (보+ㅂ니까)?

말리다 — to dry
Casual formality: 말려? (말리+어?)
Polite low formality: 말려요? (말리+어요?)
Polite high formality: 말립니까? (말리+ㅂ니까?))

하다 — to do
Casual formality: 해?
Polite low formality: 해요?
Polite high formality: 합니까? (하+ㅂ니까?)

I know what you did!

PRACTICE QUIZ

Identify which of the three formality levels the following inquisitive present form verbs belong to.

Casual Formality / Polite Low Formality / Polite High Formality

돌다 to turn

돕니까?
돌아?
돌아요?

오다 to come

와?
옵니까?
와요?

노래하다 to sing

노래해?
노래합니까?
노래해요?

긁다 to scratch

긁어?
긁어요?
긁습니까?

ANSWER: 돌다 –> 돕니까? Polite High 돌아? Casual 돌아요? Polite Low
오다 –> 와? Casual 옵니까? Polite High 와요? Polite Low
노래하다 –> 노래해? Casual 노래합니까? Polite High 노래해요? Polite Low
긁다 –> 긁어? Casual 긁어요? Polite Low 긁습니까? Polite High

Convert the following base form verbs into the three formality forms (inquisitive present).

사다 — to buy
Casual formality:

Polite low formality:

Polite high formality:

입다 — to wear
Casual formality:

Polite low formality:

Polite high formality:

먹다 — to eat
Casual formality:

Polite low formality:

Polite high formality:

ANSWER: 사다 –> 사? / 사요? / 삽니까?
입다 –> 입어? / 입어요? / 입습니까?
먹다 –> 먹어? / 먹어요? / 먹습니까?

Inquisitive Past

- Drop the 다 ending from the verb stem
- Just like present tense verbs, some verbs that end in a vowel will condense.

For example: 사다 (to buy) + 았어? becomes 샀어요? instead of 사았어요?

Casual formality

Verb (ending in ㅏ/ㅗ) + 았어?

Verb (ending anything else) 었어?

Polite low formality

Verb (ending in ㅏ/ㅗ)+ 았어요?

Verb (ending anything else) + 었어요?

Polite high formality

Verb (ending in a vowel) + 았습니까?

Verb (ending in a consonant) + 었습니까?

가다 — to go
Casual formality: 갔어? (가+았어?)
Polite low formality: 갔어요? (가+았어요?)
Polite high formality: 갔었습니까?

읽다 — to read
Casual formality: 읽었어?
Polite low formality: 읽었어요?
Polite high formality: 읽었습니까?

보다 — to see
Casual formality: 봤어? (보+았어)
Polite low formality: 봤어요? (보+았어요?)
Polite high formality: 봤습니까? (보+았습니까?)

말리다 — to dry
Casual formality: 말렸어? (말리+었어?)
Polite low formality: 말렸어요? (말리+었어요?)
Polite high formality: 말렸습니까? (말리+었습니까?)

I didn't do anything

하다 — to do
Casual formality: 했어?
Polite low formality: 했어요?
Polite high formality: 했습니까?

PRACTICE QUIZ

Identify which of the three formality levels the following inquisitive past form verbs belong to.

Casual Formality / Polite Low Formality / Polite High Formality

돌다 to turn

돌았어?
돌았습니까?
돌았어요?

오다 to come

왔어요?
왔어?
왔습니까?

노래하다 to sing

노래했어?
노래했어요?
노래했습니까?

긁다 to scratch

긁었어요?
긁었어?
긁었습니까?

ANSWER: 돌다 –> 돌았어? Casual 돌았습니까? Polite High 돌았어요? Polite Low
오다 –> 왔어요? Polite Low 왔어? Casual 왔습니까? Polite High
노래하다 –> 노래했어? Casual 노래했어요? Polite Low 노래했습니까? Polite High
긁다 –> 긁었어요? Polite Low 긁었어? Casual 긁었습니까? Polite High

Convert the following base form verbs into the three formality forms (inquisitive past).

사다 — to buy

Casual formality:

_____

Polite low formality:

_____

Polite high formality:

_____

입다 — to wear

Casual formality:

_____

Polite low formality:

_____

Polite high formality:

_____

먹다 — to eat

Casual formality:

_____

Polite low formality:

_____

Polite high formality:

_____

ANSWER: 사다 –> 샀어? / 샀어요? / 샀습니까?
입다 –> 입었어? / 입었어요? / 입었습니까?
먹다 –> 먹었어? / 먹었어요? / 먹었습니까?

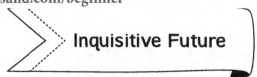

Inquisitive Future

- Drop the 다 ending from the verb stem
- If the verb ends in a vowel or 을, add ㄹ to the verb stem
- You don't need to add anything to verbs ending in ㄹ, though

---

Casual formality
Verb (ending in a vowel) + ㄹ
Verb (ending in a consonant) + 을 거야?

Polite low formality
Verb (ending in a vowel) + ㄹ
Verb (ending in a consonant) 을 거예요?

Polite high formality
Verb (ending in a vowel) + ㄹ 겁니까
Verb (ending in a consonant) + 을 겁니까?

가다 — to go
Casual formality: 갈 거야?
Polite low formality: 갈 거예요?
Polite high formality: 갈 겁니까?

읽다 — to read
Casual formality: 읽을 거야?
Polite low formality: 읽을 거예요?
Polite high formality: 읽을 겁니까?

보다 — to see
Casual formality: 볼 거야?
Polite low formality: 볼 거예요?
Polite high formality: 볼 겁니까?

말리다 — to dry
Casual formality: 말릴 거야?
Polite low formality: 말릴 거예요?
Polite high formality: 말릴 겁니까?

하다 — to do
Casual formality: 할 거야?
Polite low formality: 할 거예요?
Polite high formality: 할 겁니까?

This time 하다 follows the rule!

104

PRACTICE QUIZ

Identify which of the three formality levels the following inquisitive past form verbs belong to.

Casual Formality / Polite Low Formality / Polite High Formality

돌다 to turn

돌 겁니까?
돌 거야?
돌 거예요?

오다 to come

올 거야?
올 겁니까?
올 거예요?

노래하다 to sing

노래 할 거야?
노래 할 겁니까?
노래 할 거예요?

긁다 to scratch

긁을 겁니까?
긁을 거예요?
긁을 거야?

ANSWER: 돌다 –> 돌 겁니까? Polite High 돌 거야? Casual 돌 거예요? Polite Low
오다 –> 올 거야? Casual 올 겁니까? Polite High 올 거예요? Polite Low
노래하다 –> 노래 할 거야? Casual 노래 할 겁니까? Polite High 노래 할 거예요? Polite Low
긁다 –> 긁을 겁니까? Polite High 긁을 거예요? Polite Low 긁을 거야? Casual

Convert the following base form verbs into the three formality forms (inquisitive future).

사다 — to buy
Casual formality:

_____

Polite low formality:

_____

Polite high formality:

_____

입다 — to wear
Casual formality:

_____

Polite low formality:

_____

Polite high formality:

_____

먹다 — to eat
Casual formality:

_____

Polite low formality:

_____

Polite high formality:

_____

ANSWER: 사다 –> 살 거야? / 살 거예요? / 살 겁니까?
입다 –> 입을 거야? / 입을 거예요? / 입을 겁니까?
먹다 –> 먹을 거야? / 먹을 거예요? / 먹을 겁니까?

105

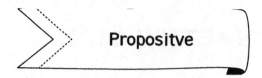

Propositve

- Drop the 다 ending from the verb stem

Casual formality
Verb (ending in ㅏ / ㅗ) + 아
Verb (ending in anything else) + 어

Polite low formality
Verb (ending in a vowel) + 세요
Verb (ending in a consonant) + 으세요

Polite high formality
Verb (ending in a vowel) + 십시오
Verb (ending in a consonant) + 으십시오

가다 — to go
Casual formality: 가
Polite low formality: 가세요
Polite high formality: 가십시오

읽다 — to read
Casual formality: 읽어
Polite low formality: 읽으세요
Polite high formality: 읽으십시오

보다 — to see
Casual formality: 봐 (보+아)
Polite low formality: 보세요
Polite high formality: 보십시오

말리다 — to dry
Casual formality: 말려 (말리+어)
Polite low formality: 말리세요
Polite high formality: 말리십시오

Shall we dance?

하다 — to do
Casual formality: 해
Polite low formality: 하세요
Polite high formality: 하십시오

PRACTICE QUIZ

Identify which of the three formality levels the following inquisitive past form verbs belong to.

Casual Formality / Polite Low Formality / Polite High Formality

돌다 to turn

돌아
도세요
도십시오

오다 to come

오세요
오십시오
와

노래하다 to sing

노래하세요
노래해
노래하십시오

긁다 to scratch

긁어
긁으십시오
긁으세요

ANSWER: 돌다 –> 돌아 Casual 도세요 Polite Low 도십시오 Polite High
오다 –> 오세요 Polite Low 오십시오 Polite High 와 Casual
노래하다 –> 노래하세요 Polite Low 노래해 Casual 노래하십시오 Polite High
긁다 –> 긁어 Casual 긁으십시오 Polite High 긁으세요 Polite Low

Convert the following base form verbs into the three formality forms (propositive).

사다 — to buy
Casual formality:

_____

Polite low formality:

_____

Polite high formality:

_____

입다 — to wear
Casual formality:

_____

Polite low formality:

_____

Polite high formality:

_____

먹다 — to eat
Casual formality:

_____

Polite low formality:

_____

Polite high formality:

_____

ANSWER: 사다 –> 사 / 사세요 / 사십시오
입다 –> 입어 / 입으세요 / 입으십시오
먹다 –> 먹어 / 먹으세요 / 먹으십시오

PASSIVE VERBS

 MP3 〈38〉

엄마가 철수를 혼냈어요
Mom scolded Cheol-su.

ACTION VERB

철수가 엄마에게 혼났어요.
Cheol-su was scolded by mom.

PASSIVE VERB

All right guys! Let's learn about passive verbs! As you know, passive verbs are about the object which an action is performed, while action verbs are about the subject which performs an action.

Pay attention to what happens when a sentence has a passive verb in it.

- Object becomes the subject.
  엄마가 철수를 혼냈어요. -> **철수가** 엄마에게 혼났어요.

- The verb changes from its active to passive form.
  혼**냈어요** (to scold) -> 혼**났어요** (to be scolded)

- The active subject becomes passive agent by which the action happens.
  〈엄마**가** -> 엄마**에게**〉 here, you can think **에게** as "by".

For **animate agent,** use **한테/에게** for casual/plain but always use **께** for polite high situations (e.g., referring to senior citizens, parents, higher in rank, and etc.)

Example)

> These also mean "to", depending on the context (e.g., 친구한테 선물을 주었다. I gave a gift to a friend). We'll learn this later.

여우가 토끼를 <u>먹었다</u>. A fox ate a rabbit

-> 토끼가 여우**한테** <u>먹혔다</u>. A rabbit was eaten by a fox.

할아버지가 도둑을 <u>쫓았다</u>. A grandpa chased a thief.

-> 도둑이 할아버지**께** <u>쫓겼다</u>. A thief was chased by a grandpa.

For **inanimate agent,** use **에**

Example)

태양이 얼음을 <u>녹였어요</u>. The sun melted ice.

-> 얼음이 태양**에** <u>녹았어요</u>. The ice was melted by the sun.

For **both animate AND inanimate agents,** you can also use **~에 의해** (due to/by). But keep in mind that sometimes it might sound awkward, depending on the context. You will learn this difference as we go on.

Example)

인부가 집을 <u>지었다</u>. A worker built a house.

-> 집이 인부에 **의해** <u>지어졌다</u>. A house was built by a worker.

생각이 세상을 <u>바꾸었다</u>. The idea changed the world.

-> 세상이 생각에 **의해** <u>바뀌었다</u>. The world was changed due to the idea.

Here are some general rules and types of passive verbs.
As usual, there are exceptions to these, but you'll get used to them as we learn more.

STEM + 어지다 / 아지다 / 지다

For adjectives,

Refer back to the verb conjugation lesson for a quick refresher!

ADJECTIVE BASE	DESCRIPTIVE VERB	PAST	PRESENT CONTINUOUS PASSIVE
높은 (high)	높아지다 (get higher)	높아졌다 (got higher)	높아지고있다 (getting higher)
아름다운 (beautiful)	아름다워지다 (get beautiful)	아름다워졌다 (got beautiful)	아름다워지고있다 (getting beautiful)

Same goes for verbs,

VERB BASE	PASSIVE BASE	PASSIVE PAST	PRESENT CONTINUOUS PASSIVE
주다 (to give)	주어지다 (to be given)	주어졌다 (was given)	주어지고있다 (being given)
켜다 (to turn on)	켜지다 (to be turned on)	켜졌다 (was turned on)	켜지고있다 (being turned on)

STEM + 이다

– For stems without 받침
– For stems with 받침 ㅎ, ㄲ, ㅍ

VERB BASE	PASSIVE BASE	PASSIVE PAST	PRESENT CONTINUOUS PASSIVE
모으다 (to gather)	모이다 (to be gathered)	모였다 (모이+었다) (was gathered)	모이고있다 (being gathered)
바꾸다 (to change)	바뀌다 (바꾸+이다) (to be changed)	바뀌었다 (was changed)	바뀌고있다 (being changed)
쌓다 (to pile up)	쌓이다 (to be piled up)	쌓였다 (was piled up)	쌓이고있다 (being piled up)
섞다 (to mix)	섞이다 (to be mixed)	섞였다 (was mixed)	섞이고있다 (being mixed)
덮다 (to cover)	덮이다 (to be covered)	덮였다 (was covered)	덮이고있다 (being covered)

STEM + 히다
– For stems with 받침 ㄱ, ㄷ, ㅂ, ㅈ

VERB BASE	PASSIVE BASE	PASSIVE PAST	PRESENT CONTINUOUS PASSIVE
읽다 (to read)	읽히다 (to be read)	읽혔다 (읽히+었다) (was read)	읽히고있다 (being read)
닫다 (to close)	닫히다 (to be closed)	닫혔다 (was closed)	닫히고있다 (being closed)
밟다 (to step on)	밟히다 (to be stepped on)	밟혔다 (was stepped on)	밟히고있다 (being stepped on)
잊다 (to forget)	잊히다 (to be forgotten)	잊혔다 (was forgotten)	잊히고있다 (being forgotten)

STEM + 리다
– For stems with 받침 ㄹ, or irregular verbs whose 받침 changes to ㄹ when conjugated (듣다 -> 들어)

VERB BASE	PASSIVE BASE	PASSIVE PAST	PRESENT CONTINUOUS PASSIVE
밀다 (to push)	밀리다 (to be pushed)	밀렸다 (was pushed)	밀리고있다 (being pushed)
듣다 (to hear)	들리다 (to be heard)	들렸다 (was heard)	들리고있다 (being heard)
부르다 (to sing)	불리다 (to be sung)	불렸다 (was sung)	불리고있다 (being sung)

STEM + 기다
– For stems with 받침 that doesn't change it's sound when it comes before ㅎ (usually ㅁ, ㄴ, ㅅ, ㅊ)

VERB BASE	PASSIVE BASE	PASSIVE PAST	PRESENT CONTINUOUS PASSIVE
감다 (to wind up)	감기다 (to be wound up)	감겼다 (감기+었다) (was wound up)	감기고있다 (being wound up)
안다 (to hug)	안기다 (to be hugged)	안겼다 (was hugged)	안기고있다 (being hugged)
빗다 (to comb)	빗기다 (to be combed)	빗겼다 (was combed)	빗기고있다 (being combed)
쫓다 (to chase)	쫓기다 (to be chased)	쫓겼다 (was chased)	쫓기고있다 (being chased)

STEM + 하다 / 되다

While 하다 describes the act, 되다 describes the object on which the action is performed.

포함<u>하다</u> (to include) vs. 포함<u>되다</u> (to be included) | 생각<u>하다</u> (to think) vs. 생각<u>되다</u> (to be thought)

새로운 그룹이 선희를 포함했다. The new group <u>included</u> Seon-hee.
선희가 새로운 그룹에 포함<u>되었다</u>. Seon-hee <u>was included</u> in the new group.

STEM + 내다 / 나다

While 내다 describes the subject who performs the act, 나다 describes the object on which the action is performed.

고장<u>내다</u> (to break) vs. 고장<u>나다</u> (to be broken) | 끝<u>내다</u> (to finish) vs. 끝<u>나다</u> (to be finished)

철수가 컴퓨터를 고장냈다. Cheol-su <u>broke</u> the computer.
컴퓨터가 고장났다. The computer <u>is broken</u> (by Cheol-su).

철수가 숙제를 끝냈다. Cheol-su <u>finished</u> the homework.
숙제가 끝났다. The homework <u>was finished</u> (by Cheol-su).

Not all words ending in 내다 have an equivalent 나다 verb (and vice-versa), nor do the words ending in 하다 have an equivalent 되다 verb (and vice-versa). For example, 돈내다 (to spend money) is a word but 돈나다 is not a word. Similarly, 공부하다 (to study) is a word but 공부되다 is not a word. You'd have to learn them on a case-by-case basis, but 내다/나다 and 하다/되다 are the most common types.

ESSENTIAL PARTICLES

Particle	Example (Korean)	Example (English)
들 (plural marker)	고양이<u>들</u>	cat<u>s</u>
만 (only)	사람들<u>만</u>	<u>only</u> humans / humans <u>only</u>
관해서 (about/regarding)	음식에 <u>관해서</u>	<u>about</u> food
위해서 (for)	너를 <u>위해서</u>	<u>for</u> you
과/와 함께 (with) (과 for word ending with batchim 와 for word ending with a vowel)	구름<u>과 함께</u> 너<u>와 함께</u>	<u>with</u> the cloud <u>with</u> you

PRACTICE QUIZ

Convert the following active sentence into passive sentence.

경찰이 도둑을 잡았다. -> _____이 _____ 에게 _____.
The police caught the thief. -> The thief was caught by the police.

코끼리가 거북이를 밟았다. -> _____가 _____ 한테 _____.
The elephant stepped on the turtle. -> The turtle was stepped on by the elephant.

ANSWER: 도둑이 경찰에게 잡혔다. / 거북이가 코끼리한테 밟혔다.

Choose between **한테/에게/께** for the following sentences.

1. 철수가 나쁜 친구_____ 맞았다.
Cheol-su was hit by a bad friend.

2. 고양이가 개_____ 물렸다.
The cat was bitten by the dog.

3. 나뭇잎이 바람_____ 날렸다.
The leaf was blown by the wind.

4. 유리가 망치_____ 깨졌다.
The glass was broken by a hammer.

Inanimate

5. 신입사원이 사장님_____ 혼났다.
The new employee was scolded by the president.

6. 학생이 젊은 선생님_____ 교육받았다.
The student was educated by the young teacher.

ANSWER: 1. 한테/에게 2. 한테/에게 3. 에 4. 에 5. 께 6. 께

Use **~에 의해** to convert the following active sentence into passive sentence.

노력이 좋은 결과를 만들었다. –> _____가 _____ 에 의해 _____.
The effort made a good result. –> A good result was made by the effort.

구름이 태양을 가렸다. –> _____이 _____ _____.
The cloud covered the sun. –> The sun was covered by the cloud.

ANSWER: 좋은 결과가 노력에 의해 만들어졌다. / 태양이 구름에 의해 가려졌다.

Choose between **하다 / 되다** to fill in the blanks.

기억_____ (to remember) vs. 기억_____ (to be remembered)
파괴_____ (to be destroyed) vs. 파괴_____ (to destroy)
수용_____ (to embrace) vs. 수용_____ (to be embraced)
거절_____ (to be rejected) vs. 거절_____ (to reject)

ANSWER: 하다 / 되다
되다 / 하다
하다 / 되다
되다 / 하다

Choose between **내다 / 나다** to fill in the blanks.

혼_____ (to be scolded) vs. 혼_____ (to scold)
드러_____ (to be exposed) vs. 드러_____ (to expose)
나타_____ (to appear) vs. 나타_____ (to be appeared)

ANSWER: 나다/내다
나다/내다
내다/나다

PLACE/SPACE
~에서/~부터 & ~까지

How long would it take **from** Seoul **to** Busan?
I should go to bed early.

I slept **from** yesterday **until** now!

As you can see, the same English particle **FROM** has two variations in Korean, which are **부터** and **에서**.

As a rule of thumb, **부터** is often used for **TIME**, while **에서** is used for **PLACE**.

But most of the time they are **interchangeable**, as illustrated below.

PLACE	TIME
FROM here **TO** there	**FROM** SUNDAY **TO** MONDAY
여기**에서** 저기**까지** (o)	일요일**부터** 월요일**까지** (o)
여기**부터** 저기**까지** (o)	일요일**에서** 월요일**까지** (o)

Then let's learn **when they are and are not interchangeable.**

First of all, exceptions occur when you talk about **TIME.**

When you talk about specific time with numbers, like 2시 (two o'clock), 5월 ("Month Five" = May), or specific year like 2021년, or specific date of the week like 일요일 (Sunday), or specific date in a month like 19일 (19th day / day 19th, you can use 부터 and 에서 interchangeably.

✓ 일요일**부터** 월요일**까지**
From Sunday **to** Monday.

✓ 일요일**에서** 월요일**까지**
From Sunday **to** Monday.

Why can the days of the week, despite not having a number, use both 부터 and 에서? It's because just like the months of the year, for example, May, it's treated as a number. That's why it's 5월 ("5th Month") in Korean. Same goes for specific days of the week. 월요일 (Monday) is treated like "First day of the week", even though it doesn't literally say that. It's assumed. Hence this rule doesn't apply here.

Conversely, when you talk about the time without numbers like 작년 (last year), 어제 (yesterday), then you should only use 부터. Also, when you use words like 전 (before) / 후 (after) / 지나서 (past), you use 부터 only, even when there's a specific number. See the examples below.

✓ 어제**부터** 오늘**까지** 공부했다.
(I) studied **from** yesterday **until** today.

✗ 어제**에서** 오늘**까지** 공부했다.
(I) studied **from** yesterday **until** today.

✓ 2010년전**부터** 2019년**까지**
From <u>before</u> year 2010 to <u>year</u> 2019

✗ 2010년전**에서** 2019년**까지**
From <u>before</u> year 2010 to <u>year</u> 2019

Let's look at some examples to help you understand.

NOUN + 에서 = PLACE		
	미국에서 한국까지.	From the U.S. to Korea.
	학교에서 집까지 .	From school to home.
a	9시에서 10시까지	From nine o'clock to ten o'clock
b	10살에서 11살까지	From age 10 to age 11
c	3번째 페이지에서 9번째 페이지까지	From the 3rd page to the 9th page.

NOUN + 부터 = TIME		
	어제부터 내일까지	From yesterday to tomorrow.
	언제부터 언제까지?	From when to when?
a	9시부터 10시까지	From nine o'clock to ten o'clock
b	10살부터 11살까지	From age 10 to age 11
c	3번째 페이지부터 9번째 페이지까지	From the 3rd page to the 9th page.

You can clearly see their uses as well as when they are (example a,b,c are) and aren't interchangeable.

And 까지 is used to mean both TO (PLACE) and TO / UNTIL (TIME & PLACE) / BY (TIME ONLY).

NOUN + 까지 = TO / UNTIL (TIME & PLACE) / BY (TIME ONLY)	
토요일까지 공부 할겁니다.	I will study **until** Saturday.
뉴욕까지 얼마나 걸립니까?	How long does it take **to** New York?
내일까지 하겠습니다.	I will do it **by** tomorrow.

PRACTICE QUIZ

Fill in the blanks with either 에서 / 부터 or BOTH

1. 오늘_____ 내일까지 잠 잘거야.
(I) will sleep from today until tomorrow.

2. 여기_____ 거기까지 몇 시간 걸리나요?
From here to there, how many hours does it take?

3. 지금_____ 저녁까지 뭐 할 거예요?
From now to tonight, what are you going to do?

4. 어렸을 때 _____ 지금까지, 우유를 사랑합니다.
From when I was little until now, I love milk.

5. 공항_____ 호텔까지 몇 시간 걸리나요?
From the airport to the hotel, how many hours does it take?

6. 3시_____ 5시까지 운동 할 거예요.
(I) will work out from three o'clock to five o'clock.

7. 2번째 페이지_____ 34번째 페이지까지.
From the 2nd page to the 34th page.

ANSWER: 1. 부터 2. 에서 3. 부터 4. 부터 5. 에서 6. BOTH 7. BOTH

Read the sentences and see whether 에서 / 부터 is used correctly (O) or not (X).

1. 서울<u>부터</u> 부산까지 5시간 걸려요.
From Seoul to Busan, it takes five hours.

2. 지금<u>에서</u> 아침까지 기다릴게요.
From now to morning, I will wait.

3. 내일<u>부터</u> 모레까지!
From tomorrow until the day after tomorrow!

4. 4시<u>에서</u> 11시까지!
From four o'clock to 11 o'clock!

ANSWER: 1. X 2. X 3. O 4. O

NUMBERS IN KOREAN

One, two, three… We all wish learning Korean were as easy as counting numbers, right? But you might want to hold that idea because… there are two ways to count numbers in Korean!

What…? I'm having a headache again… ugh!

Don't worry! You will get the hang of it before even you know it!.

A little background about this: Korean words have what's called Sino—Korean words and pure Korean words. The former refers to words that are based on Traditional Chinese characters because Korea, in the past, didn't have its own writing system and had to rely on the Chinese system. As a result, Korean people adopted lots of vocabulary words based on it. But because Korean people had their own way of reading them, the pronunciation is different from that of the Chinese people.

漢字　우리말

Oh, and don't worry — there's no need for you to learn the Chinese characters because they are all transcribed with the Korean alphabet, Hangul (King Sejong the Great invented a unique set of alphabet system, which we learned at the beginning of the book, in 1443).

With the quick history lesson out of the way, let's start counting numbers in Korean!

	Sino-Korean			Pure Korean	
0	영 (공)				
1	일			하나	
2	이			둘	
3	삼			셋	
4	사			넷	
5	오			다섯	
6	육			여섯	
7	칠			일곱	
8	팔			여덟	
9	구			아홉	
10	십			열	
11	십일	십+일 (10) + (1)		열하나	열+하나 (10) + (1)
12	십이	십+이 (10) + (2)		열둘	열+둘 (10) + (2)
13	십삼	십+삼 (10) + (3)		열셋	열+셋 (10) + (3)
14	십사	십+사 (10) + (4)		열넷	열+넷 (10) + (4)
15	십오	십+오 (10) + (5)		열다섯	열+다섯 (10) + (5)
20	이십	이+십 (2)+ (10) **twen+TY**		스물	
21	이십일	이십+일 (20) + (1) **twenty + one**		스물하나	스물+하나 (20) + (1)
30	삼십	삼+십 (3) + (10) **thir+TY**		서른	
40	사십	사+십 (4) + (10) **for+TY**		마흔	
50	오십	오+십 (5) + (10) **fif+TY**		쉰	
60	육십	육+십 (6) + (10) **six+TY**		예순	
70	칠십	칠+십 (7) + (10) **seven+TY**		일흔	
80	팔십	팔+십 (8) + (10) **eigh+TY**		여든	
90	구십	구+십 (9) + (10) **nin+TY**		아흔	
100	백			온	
1,000	천			즈믄	
10,000	만			골	
100,000	십만	십+만 (10) + (10,000)		열골/열거믄	
1,000,000	백만			온골/온거믄	

Sino–Korean Numbers

Knowing **0–10** is half the job done because it's just about putting the tenth digit and the single digit together!

11 십일 (10) + (1)

12 십이 (10) + (2)

13 십삼 (10) + (3)

14 십사 (10) + (4)

tenth digit single digit

Notice on the chart that every tenth mark, the word for the tenth digit changes in the same order of **1–9**, followed by the word 십 **10.** In fact, it's exactly the same as English!

20 twenty is 이십 (이 two + 십 ten) –> two+ten = twen+ty

30 thirty is 삼십 (삼 three + 십 ten) –> three+ten = thir+ty

40 forty is 사십 (사 four + 십 ten) –> four+ten = for+ty

hence,

21 이십일 (20) + (1)

34 삼십사 (30) + (4)

And 100 백 is a unique word, instead of 십십 10+10.
And so on
Same goes for **1,000** 천 and **10,000** 만.

200 이백 (2) + (100)

340 삼백사십 (3 + 100) + (4 + 10)

592 오백구십이 (5 + 100) + (9 + 10) + (2)

123

Now, when numbers are transcribed in Korean, spacing takes place with every 만 unit.

6,132 육천백삼십이 (6 + 1,000) + (1 + 100) + (3 + 10) + (2)

78,232 칠만 팔천이백삼십이 (7 + 10,000) + (8 + 1000) + (2 + 100) + (3 + 10) + (2)

*When numbers are transcribed in Korean, spacing takes place with every 만 unit.

칠만팔천이백삼십이 (x) 칠만 ∧ 팔천이백삼십이 (o)

Just like how **10** served as the basis mark for 10, 20, 30… to 90,

now 만 10,000 does the same for 100,000 and 1,000,000, and 10,000,000.

i.e., "How many 'ten thousands'?"

That is,

10,000 만 (ten thousand = '1 ten thousand') / 100,000 십만 (ten + ten thousand)

1,000,000 백만 (hundred + ten thousand) / 10,000,000 천만 (thousand + ten thousand)

This can be quite confusing because English counting convention puts a comma at every third digit from the right

(1,000, 1,000,000, etc.)

10,000 ten THOUSAND / 100,000 hundred THOUSAND

So it's easier to think that Koreans are putting a comma before every four zeros, and read it 만.

For example,

1,0000 만 / 10,0000 십만 you get the idea!

Now, let's read some BIG NUMBERS!

83,924,315 팔천삼백구십이만 사천삼백십오

Technically, it's 일백 / 일천 / 일만 / 일십만 for 100 / 1000 / 10000 / 100000, but colloquially, it's often said as 백 / 천 / 만 / 십만 … so instead of "One Hundred", it's "Hundred", and so on.

But on official documents such as a contract, it is spelled out for accuracy.

Pure-Korean Numbers

Pure-Korean numbers are quite easy to master as well because it's about putting numbers together as well, and you really just need to know the numbers from 1-99. This is because there's no word for 0 in pure Korean. As for numbers 100 and beyond, there are archaic pure Korean words that are almost never used (less work for us, yay!).

This is very important because beyond 100, Sino-Korean numbers are used for counting, even for those counted with pure Korean counter words (more details on the next page).

Looking at the chart, we can quickly learn 1 to 10.

And from 11 to 19, it's exactly the same because you basically add:

열하나 (10) + (1) 열둘 (10) + (2) 열셋 (10) + (3) and so on.

Now you just need to learn the tens, which don't have a particular set of rules and have their own names.

That is,

Instead of 둘열, it's 스물.
Instead of 셋열, it's 서른.
Instead of 넷열, it's 마흔.

Just memorize them as there are only 9 of them!

But again, combined numbers like 13, 25, 39, 54 are the same as Sino-Korean numbers.

13 열셋 (10) + (3)
25 스물다섯 (20) + (5)
39 서른아홉 (30) + (9)
54 쉰넷 (50) + (4)

125

Okay! Now with that out of the way, let's learn when to use which! But before we continue, there's a very important concept you need to know, which is 'counter word'. In Korean, when counting, words have a specific 'counter word' after the subject/object. And here are the common examples.

	Sino-Korean		Pure-Korean	
Days	일	삼일 (three days)		*
Months	월	삼월 (month 3 = March)		
Month (Duration)	개월	일개월 (one month)	달	한 달 (one month)
Years	년	이년 (two years/year 2)	해	두 해 (two years)
Time	분	삼 분 (three minutes)	시	세 시 (three o'clock)
People/Person	인	십일인 (eleven people)	명/분	열한 명 (eleven people) 열한 분 (eleven people, honorific)
Floor(s)	층	일층 (floor one)	층	한 층 (one floor)
Things			개	OOO 네 개 (four ooo's)
Animals			마리	개 다섯 마리 (five dogs)
Slices			조각	피자 여섯 조각 (six slices of pizza)
Books			권	책 일곱 권 (seven books)
Clothes			벌	정장 여덟 벌 (eight suits)
Papers/Sheets			장	아홉 장 (nine sheets)
Vehicles			대	비행기 열 대 (ten airplanes)

As briefly mentioned before, when the number goes above **100**, Sino–Korean numbers are used for counting. even with the ones that use Pure–Korean counter words, because Pure–Korean numbers go only up to **99**.

For example,

아흔 아홉 대 ninety–nine vehicles vs. 백삼십사 대 one–hundred and thirty–four vehicles
열세 명 thirteen people vs. 이백삼십사 명 two–hundred and thirty–four people

A few things to note here.

When counting using Pure-Korean numbers, the following five numbers change the form when used
BEFORE a counter word.

하나 –› 한 / 둘 –› 두 / 셋 –› 세 / 넷 –› 네 / 스물 –› 스무

For example,

강아지 **하나** "one dog" <– when the counter word 마리 isn't used (grammatically incorrect but still makes sense).
vs.
강아지 **한** 마리 <– here, 마리 is correctly used and 하나 becomes 한 and comes before the counter word 마리.

Similarly, you could say 어른 하나 ("one adult"), 피자 다섯 ("five pizzas"), without proper counter words,
어른 한 명 ("one adult person") and 피자 다섯 조각 ("five pizza slices"), and still make sense.

It's similar to saying "We'll have five waters." Technically incorrect, but still makes sense.
Just keep in mind how the forms change 하나 –› 한, 둘 –› 두, and so on.

• In English, the words such as days, months, years, minutes, hours, people/person floor, slices are counter words,
so you shouldn't have a problem understanding the concept. What might confuse you are, though, the other types of
counter words, such as 마리 for animals, 권 for books, and 대 for vehicles because such subjects/objects don't have
a specific counter word.

That is, you wouldn't say "ten airplane vehicles" but say "ten airplanes". In Korean, it's 대,
so 비행기 열 대 is "ten airplane vehicles".

Same goes for 마리 for animals,
You wouldn't say "five dogs animals", but say "five dogs". No specific counter word for animals, either (but of course,
there are terms like "school of fish", but not in general).

So 개 다섯 마리 is "five dogs animals" in Korean. It might sound weird, but just know that it's exactly the same
concept as the other counter words in English. ("Six pizzas" vs. "six slices of pizza")

Looking at the chart, there are some counter words that are used for both Sino-Korean AND pure-Korean, such as 층.

But notice they can have different meanings – 일층 means "floor one", describing the location while 한 층 means "one floor", describing quantity. Another example (not on the chart) is 번, used for numbers.

일번 means "number one", while 한 번 means "one time = once". So some words, while interchangeable, might have completely different meanings, so be on the look out for that. But you don't need to memorize them as if you were preparing for a test. You will pick them up as we progress!

A: Excuse me! Where's the bathroom?
B: Go up to floor 9.

A: Excuse me! Where's the bathroom?
B: Go up 9 floors.

For pure-Korean, the days/months sections are left blank,
because they don't follow the general rule described in the table chart and require a separate table for them.

	Sino-Korean	Pure-Korean
January	일월	정월
February	이월	
March	삼월	
April	사월	
May	오월	
June	유월	
July	칠월	
August	팔월	
September	구월	
October	시월	
November	십일월	동짓달
December	십이월	섣달

*Technically, 육월/십월 are correct, but they've become 유월/시월 because they are easier to pronounce.

Counting Days in Pure-Korean			
Day 1 / 1 Day	초하루 / 하루	Day 16 / 16 Days	열엿새
Day 2 / 2 Days	이틀	Day 17 / 17 Days	열이레
Day 3 / 3 Days	사흘	Day 18 / 18 Days	열여드레
Day 4 / 4 Days	나흘	Day 19 / 19 Days	열아흐레
Day 5 / 5 Days	닷새	Day 20 / 20 Days	스무날
Day 6 / 6 Days	엿새	Day 21 / 21 Days	스무하루
Day 7 / 7 Days	이레	Day 22 / 22 Days	스무이틀
Day 8 / 8 Days	여드레	Day 23 / 23 Days	스무사흘
Day 9 / 9 Days	아흐레	Day 24 / 24 Days	스무나흘
Day 10 / 10 Days	열흘	Day 25 / 25 Days	스무닷새
Day 11 / 11 Days	열하루	Day 26 / 26 Days	스무엿새
Day 12 / 12 Days	열이틀	Day 27 / 27 Days	스무이레
Day 13 / 13 Days	열사흘	Day 28 / 28 Days	스무여드레
Day 14 / 14 Days	열나흘	Day 29 / 29 Days	스무아흐레
Day 15 / 15 Days	열닷새 (보름)	Day 30 / 30 Days	그믐
		Day 31	n/a because lunar calendar system doesn't have 31st day

Okay, so when to use which?

Sino-Korean numbers

These are 'counter words'

Saying The Date
일월 일일 (Month 1, Day 1 = January 1st)

Saying specific Numbers (Phone numbers, apartment unit numbers, and etc.)

이이일-삼일삼사 (221-3134)
십육동 **이십삼**호 (Building #16, Unit #23)

Counting The Days
일일 (1 day / one day), **이**일 (2 days / day 2), **삼**일 (3 days / day 3)

Counting The Years
일년 (one year / year 1) **이**년 (two years / year 2), **이천이십**년 (2020 years / year 2020)

Counting The Months
일 개월 (1 month),

Counting Money
삼만 구천원 (39,000 Won)

Pure-Korean numbers

When counting things that are not mentioned above and are not interchangeable with the Sino-Korean words.

조약돌 **하나** "one pebble" 조약돌 **한** 개 "one pebble thing"

'counter word' right here

PRACTICE QUIZ

Which of the following are Sino-Korean numbers?

하나 / 이 / 셋 / 넷 / 오 / 육 / 일곱 / 여덟 / 구 / 열

ANSWER: 이 / 오 / 육 / 구

Which of the following are Pure-Korean numbers?

십 / 열 / 십일 / 열둘 / 십삼 / 열여섯 / 이십 / 스물

ANSWER: 열 / 열둘 / 열여섯 / 스물

Write the following numbers using Sino-Korean numbers.

8 / 39 / 88 / 93 / 100 / 115 / 831

ANSWER: 팔 / 삼십구 / 팔십팔 / 구십삼 / (일)백 / (일)백십오 / 팔백삼십일

Write the following numbers using Pure-Korean numbers.

8 / 39 / 88 / 93 / 100 / 115 / 831

ANSWER: 여덟 / 서른아홉 / 아흔셋 / NA / NA / NA

For the following English sentences, choose the correct translation.

3 days	삼일 ı 사흘 ı BOTH		**3 months**	삼개월 ı 세 달 ı BOTH
3 years	삼년 ı 세 해 ı BOTH		**floor #1**	일층 ı 한 층 ı BOTH
9 dogs	개 구 마리 ı 개 아홉 마리 ı BOTH		**5 books**	책 오 권 ı 책 다섯 권 ı BOTH

ANSWER: BOTH / BOTH / BOTH / 일층 / 개 아홉 마리 / 책 다섯 권

For the following, choose the correct counter words.

15 birds	새 다섯 (　)	**3 slices of bread**	빵 세 (　)
20 sheets of paper	종이 스무 (　)	**8 bicycles**	자전거 여덟 (　)

ANSWER: 마리 / 조각 / 장 / 대

Telling Time in Korean

All right! Thanks to the hard training we've had on counting numbers, we can easily learn how to tell time in Korean. You just need to know the counter words,

시 for hour / 분 for minute / 초 for second

and the rule that the
hour takes **Pure-Korean** numbers
minute and **second** take **Sino-Korean** numbers!

| Pure-Korean numbers | | Sino-Korean numbers |

For example, the time above is

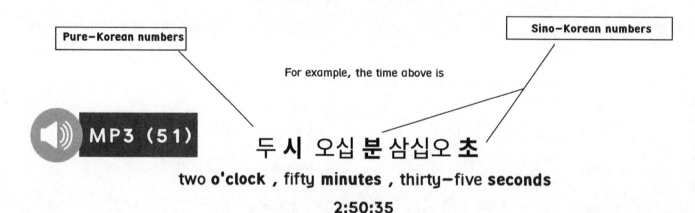

두 시 오십 분 삼십오 초

two **o'clock** , fifty **minutes** , thirty-five **seconds**

2:50:35

MP3 (51)

Another example –

다섯 시 사십 분 오 초
five **o'clock** , forty **minutes** , five **seconds**
5:40:05

You might be wondering if there are other ways to tell time, like "quarter to five" or "half past ten" in English? There is, but there's no "quarter", and just "before" and "half" are used.

전 before / to : 여섯 시 십오 분 전 <- 15 minutes before six o'clock (= no "quarter" to six)

반 half : 일곱 시 반 <- "half" past seven.

"Half" is never used alone to mean "thirty minutes" before / to, but can be used in conjunction with 시간 "hour".

i.e., 반 전 세 시 "half before three o'clock" (X) <- can't be used alone

the "target time" is placed in the end

두 시간 반 전 세 시 (o)

When counting hours, it's 시간, not 시

And yes, it's perfectly fine to use "삼십 분" instead of "half".

세 시 삼십 분 전

Ways of Telling Time

정각 (just / sharp)
세 시 **정각**
Three o'clock sharp.

오전 (in the morning)
오전 9시
Nine o'clock in the morning.

정오 (midday)

12:00 PM

오후 (in the afternoon)
오후 9시
Nine o'clock in the evening.

"오" means "day/day time" in Sino-Korean, so 오전 (AM) is "before day" and 오후 (PM) is "after day"

PRACTICE QUIZ

What time is it? Write the time shown below each clock in Korean.

ANSWER: 여덟 시 오십 분 / 여덟 시 십 분 / 한 시 사십오 분

Draw the minute / hour hands of the clock.

| 한 **시** 사십 분 | 네 **시** 삼십 분 | 두 **시** 삼십오 분 |

ANSWER:

Write the time shown in Korean using **반 / 정각**

Write the time shown in Korean using **전**

 ____ **시** ____ **분 전**   OR   ____ **분 전** ____ **시**

 ____ **시** ____ **분 전**   OR   ____ **분 전** ____ **시**

TYPES OF SENTENCES
Explaining & Describing

When explaining and describing what something is ("to be = is/am/are"),

add after a subject/object the following for **positive** sentences

~입니다. (formal / public / high polite)

~다 / 이다. (formal / plain / impolite)

<u>(It's) a dog.</u>

강아지**입니다**. (formal / public / polite)

강아지**다**. (formal / plain / impolite)

<u>(It's) a hand.</u>

손**입니다**. (formal / public / polite)

손**이다**. (formal / plain / impolite)

(formal / public / polite)

My name is Tony.

I am a boy.

I am three years old.

(formal / plain / impolite)

I am a genius.

I am orange in color.

I am a triangle.

PRACTICE QUIZ

Using the following words, make positive sentences that explain/describe a subject/object.

나(I) / 학생 (student) – (Formal / Public / Polite) _____

– (Formal / Plain / Impolite) _____

영희 (Yeong-hee) / 세 살 (three years old) – (Formal / Public / Polite) _____

– (Formal / Plain / Impolite) _____

ANSWER: 나는 학생입니다. / 나는 학생이다. / 영희는 세 살입니다. / 영희는 세 살이다.

add after a subject/object the following for **negative** sentences

~〈이/가〉 **아닙니다.**
~〈이/가〉 **아니다.**

(It's) not a dog.

강아지가 **아닙니다.** (formal / public / polite)
강아지가 **아니다.** (formal / plain / impolite)

(It's) not a hand.

손이 **아닙니다.** (formal / public / polite)
손이 **아니다.** (formal / plain / impolite)

(formal / public / polite)

저는 Tony**가 아닙니다.**
저는 남자**가 아닙니다.**
세 **살이 아닙니다.**

My name **is not** Tony.
I **am not** a boy.
I **am not** three years old.

(formal / plain / impolite)

나는 천재**가 아니다**
나는 주황색**이 아니다.**
나는 삼각형**이 아니다.**

I **am not** a genius.
I **am not** orange in color.
I **am not** a triangle.

PRACTICE QUIZ

Using the following words, make negative sentences that explain/describe a subject/object.

나(I) / 학생 (student) – (Formal / Public / Polite) _____
– (Formal / Plain / Impolite) _____

영희 (Yeong-hee) / 세 살 (three years old) – (Formal / Public / Polite) _____
– (Formal / Plain / Impolite) _____

ANSWER: 나는 학생이 아닙니다. / 나는 학생이 아니다. / 영희는 세살이 아닙니다. / 영희는 세살이 아니다.

Negative / Negation

안 / ~지 않다

There are two ways to negate a sentence, which can be used interchangeably. Let's learn how they are different.

 **MP3 (55)**   Base sentence : 김밥을 먹었다. I ate kimbap.

① Add **안** which acts <u>before</u> verb / adjective to negate a sentence.

김밥을 안 먹었다. I <u>not</u> ate kimbap.

-> With this, all you do is just insert "안" before the verb 먹었다 to negate the action.

② Alternatively, you can add **~지 않다** to the <u>stem</u> of verb / adjective to negate a sentence.

김밥을 먹지 않았다. I <u>did not eat</u> kimbap.

-> With this, you are conjugating the verb / adjective.

Which to choose is totally up to you, and they mean the same.

How about this?

김밥을 안 먹<u>지않았다</u>.

I <u>not</u> <u>did not eat</u> kimbap. = I ate kimbap.

Double negative, is positive. Just throwing this out here to give you an idea of how they work.

그 영화 봤어?
Have you seen the movie?

아직 안봤어!
I haven't seen it yet!

우리는 왜 날지 않아요?
How come we don't fly?

어떤 새들은 날지 않아.
Some birds don't fly.

138

PRACTICE QUIZ

Using both 안 or ~지 않다, convert the following positive sentences into negative sentences.

날씨가 덥다 The weather is hot. –> _____ the weather is not hot.

_____ the weather is not hot.

그 현실이 놀랍다! The reality is surprising! –> _____ The reality is not surprising!

_____ The reality is not surprising!

거북이는 느리다 The turtle is slow. –> _____ The turtle is not slow.

_____ The turtle is not slow.

물이 맑다 Water is clear. –> _____ Water is not clear.

_____ Water is not clear.

ANSWER: 날씨가 안 덥다. 날씨가 덥지 않다. / 그 현실이 안 놀랍다. 그 현실이 놀랍지 않다.
거북이는 안 느리다. 거북이는 느리지 않다. / 물이 안 맑다. 물이 맑지 않다.

 **MP3 〈56〉**

Choosing Between Options

~(이)나 with a noun

OR

강아지나 고양이

A dog _or_ a cat

~나 when it ends with a vowel

OR

책이나 잡지

A book _or_ a magazine

~이나 when it ends with a consonant

PRACTICE QUIZ

Use either ~이 / ~나 for the following subject

발 (foot) ____ 손 (hand)   비 (rain) _____ 눈 (snow)

소리 (sound) _____ 냄새 (smell)   불 (fire) _____ 물 (water)

ANSWER: 발이나 손 / 비나 눈/ 소리나 냄새 / 불이나 물

 **MP3 ⟨57⟩**

~거나 with a verb / adjective

Add ~거나 to a verb / adjective stem

OR

마시거나 먹거나

To drink or to eat

*(마시다 to drink) *(먹다 to eat)

맵거나 짜거나

Spicy or salty

*(맵다 is spicy) *(짜다 is salty)

PRACTICE QUIZ

Convert the following verbs / adjectives into ~거나 form.

입다 (to wear) & 벗다 (to take off) –>_____

걷다 (to walk) & 뛰다 (to run) –> _____

많다 (is plenty) & 적다 (is insufficient) –> _____

가볍다 (is light) & 무겁다 (is heavy) –> _____

ANSWER: 입거나 벗거나 / 걷거나 뛰거나 / 많거나 적거나 / 가볍거나 무겁거나

 **MP3 〈58〉**

COMPARATIVE

~보다 & 더 / 덜

> ### A 보다 B 가 더 / 덜 ADJECTIVE
> *보다 is **not** the verb meaning see/watch

B is more / less ADJECTIVE than A

For example,

장미 보다 튤립이 더 예쁘다.

Tulips are more pretty **than** roses.

장미 보다 튤립이 덜 예쁘다.

Tulips are less pretty **than** roses.

나**보다** 철수가 더 똑똑하다. I'm more smart **than** Cheol-su.

나**보다** 철수가 덜 똑똑하다. I'm less smart **than** Cheol-su.

생각**보다** 술을 더 마셨다. I drank more alcohol **than** I thought.

생각**보다** 술을 덜 마셨다. I drank less alcohol **than** I thought.

142

PRACTICE QUIZ

Using 보다 and 더 / 덜, translate the following English sentences into Korean.

그릇 (bowl) / 뜨겁다 (is hot) / 컵 (cup)

The bowl is hotter than the cup.

-> _____

The cup is less hot than the cup.

-> _____

오늘의 (today's) / 뉴스 (news) / 놀랍다 (is surprising) / 어제의 (yesterday's)

Today's news is more surprising than yesterday's news.

-> _____

Yesterday's news is less surprising than today's news.

-> _____

거북이 (turtle) / 느리다 (is slow) / 달팽이 (snail)

The turtle is more slow (= slower) than the snail.

-> _____

The snail is less slower than the turtle.

-> _____

얼음 (ice) / 맑다 (is clear) / 우유 (milk)

Ice is more clear (= clearer) than milk.

-> _____

Milk is less clear than ice.

-> _____

ANSWER: 그릇이 컵보다 더 뜨겁다. 컵이 그릇보다 덜 뜨겁다.
오늘의 뉴스가 어제의 뉴스보다 더 놀랍다. 어제의 뉴스가 오늘의 뉴스보다 덜 놀랍다.
거북이가 달팽이보다 더 느리다. 달팽이가 거북이보다 덜 느리다.
얼음이 우유보다 맑다. 우유가 얼음보다 덜 맑다.

Exclamative Sentence (Exclamation)

~구나! / ~(ㄹ)수가!

The rule is very simple! Just add ~**구나!** or ~**(ㄹ)수가** to the adjective stem to make an exclamative sentence:

~**구나!** example

예쁘다 is pretty –> 예쁘<u>구나</u>! how pretty!

아름답다 is beautiful –> 아름답<u>구나</u>! how beautiful!

정말 훌륭하<u>구나</u>!

(It's) really great! = How great!

맛있<u>구나</u>!

(It's) delicious! = How delicious!

빠르<u>구나</u>!

(You're) fast! = How fast!

PRACTICE QUIZ

Convert the following adjectives into exclamative sentences.

덥다 (is hot) –> _____

놀랍다 (is surprising) –> _____

느리다 (is slow) –> _____

맑다 (is clear) –> _____

뿌옇다 (is cloudy) –> _____

ANSWER: 덥구나! / 놀랍구나! / 느리구나! / 맑구나! / 뿌옇구나!

144

similarly, add ~(ㄹ)수가 to the adjective stem to mean the following:

예쁘다 is pretty -> 예쁠수가 (예쁘+ㄹ수가)! how <u>can be</u> pretty!

아름답다 is beautiful -> 아름다울수가! 아름답울수가 (X) how <u>can be</u> beautiful!

*for adjectives ending with a ㅂ batchim, the ㅂ is eliminated

But for ~(ㄹ) 수가! expressions, the meaning is incomplete without one of the following to complement them (reason why <u>can be</u> is underscored).

이렇게 like this / 저렇게 like that / 그렇게 like it (that)

예쁘다 is pretty -> 이렇게/저렇게/그렇게 예쁠수가 (예쁘+ㄹ수가)! how can be pretty (like this/that/it)!

아름답다 is beautiful -> 이렇게/저렇게/그렇게 아름다울수가! how can be beautiful (like this/that/it)!

저렇게 멍청할수가!

How can (subject) be that stupid!

이렇게 행복할수가!

How can (I) be this happy!

그렇게 착할수가!

How can (he/she/they) be so kind?

PRACTICE QUIZ

Convert the following adjectives into exclamative sentences using ~(ㄹ)수가!

덥다 (is hot) -> _____

놀랍다 (is surprising) -> _____

느리다 (is slow) -> _____

맑다 (is clear) -> _____

뿌옇다 (is cloudy) -> _____

ANSWER: 더울수가! / 놀라울수가! / 느릴수가! / 맑을수가! / 뿌열수가!

Wishing/Hoping

~(으)면 좋겠다

Add ~(으)면 좋겠다 to verb / adjective stem to mean "I'd like it if..."

For example,

예쁘다 is pretty –> **예쁘면 좋겠다**! I'd like it if it's pretty. = I wish/hope it's pretty.

보다 to see –> **보면 좋겠다**! I'd like it if you see it. = I wish/hope you see it.

먹다 to eat –> **먹으면 좋겠다**! I'd like it if you eat it. = I wish/hope you eat it.

There's a new movie and
I'd like it if you watch it with me!

I hope it's fun!

PRACTICE QUIZ

Convert the following verbs / adjectives into wishing / hoping form using ~(으)면 좋겠다.

먹다 to eat –> _____ wish/hope (I) can eat

놀다 to play –> _____ wish/hope (I) can play

주다 to give –> _____ wish/hope (I) can give

구르다 to roll –> _____ wish/hope (I) can roll

더럽다 is dirty –> _____ wish/hope (it) is dirty

크다 is big –> _____ wish/hope (it) is big

ANSWER: 먹으면 좋겠다. / 놀면 좋겠다. / 주면 좋겠다. / 구르면 좋겠다. / 더러우면 좋겠다. / 크면 좋겠다.

 **MP3 (62)** # Resolution/Determination

~아/어야 한다

Add **~아/어야 한다** to verb / adjective stem to mean "must/got to (be)"

For example,

보다 to see –> **봐야 한다** (보+아야 한다) (subject) must/got to see/watch

날다 to fly–> **날아야 한다** (subject) must/got to fly

먹다 to eat –> **먹어야 한다** (subject) must/got to eat

예쁘다 is pretty –> **예뻐야 한다** (예쁘 + 어야 한다) (subject) must/got to be pretty

맵다 is spicy –> **매워야 한다** (매+우어야 한다 *irregular conjugation) (food) must/got to be spicy

나는 지금 **일어나**야 한다.
I _have to_ **wake up** now.

나는 집에 **가**야 한다.
I _have to_ **go** home

PRACTICE QUIZ

Add **~아야/어야 한다** to verb / adjective stems to mean "must/got to (be)".

놀다 to play –> _____ must/got to play

입다 to wear –> _____ must/got to wear

구르다 to roll –> _____ must/got to roll

더럽다 is dirty –> _____ must/got to be dirty

크다 is big –> _____ must/got to be big

ANSWER: 놀아야 한다. / 입어야 한다. / 굴러야 한다. / 더러워야 한다. / 커야 한다.

Permission

~아/어 도 된다 / ~(으)면 안된다

Add **~아/어 도 된다** to verb / adjective stem to mean "to be allowed to" = "it's okay to" = "may"

For example,

보다 to see –> **봐도 된다 (보+아도 된다)**. (Subject) is/am/are allowed to see (it).

날다 to fly–> **날아도 된다**. (Subject) is/am/are allowed to fly.

먹다 to eat –> **먹어도 된다**. (Subject) is/am/are allowed to eat.

예쁘다 is pretty –> **예뻐도 된다**. (예쁘+어도) (Subject) is/am/are allowed to be pretty.

맵다 is spicy –> **매워도 된다** (매+우어도= 매워도 *irregular conjugation) (Food) is allowed to be spicy.

오늘은 늦게 일어나도 된다.

It's okay to get up late today.
= (Subject) may get up late today.

저녁에 사과를 먹어도 된다.

It's okay to eat an apple at night.
= (Subject) may eat an apple at night.

PRACTICE QUIZ

Convert the following verbs / adjectives to describe permission using ~아/어도 된다.

놀다 to play –> _____ allowed to/may play

입다 to wear –> _____ allowed to/may wear

구르다 to roll –> _____ allowed to/may roll

더럽다 is dirty –> _____ allowed to/may be dirty

크다 is big –> _____ allowed to/may be big

ANSWER: 놀아도 된다. / 입어도 된다. / 굴러도 된다. / 더러워도 된다. / 커 (크+어)도 된다.

Add ~(으)면 안된다 to verb / adjective stem to mean "to be not allowed to" = "it's not okay to" = "may not"

For example,

보다 to see –> **보면 안된다.** (Subject) is/am/are not allowed to see (it).

날다 to fly–> **날면 안된다.** (Subject) is/am/are not allowed to fly.

먹다 to eat –> **먹으면 안된다.** (Subject) is/am/are not allowed to eat.

예쁘다 is pretty –> **예쁘면 안된다.** (Subject) is/am/are not allowed to be pretty.

맵다 is spicy –> **매우면 안된다.** (*irregular conjugation) (Food) is not allowed to be pretty.

쓰레기를 <u>버리면 안된다</u>.

<u>It's not okay to throw away</u> the trash.

= (Subject) <u>may not throw away</u> the trash.

눈을 <u>뜨면 안된다</u>.

<u>It's not okay to open</u> your eyes.

= (Subject) <u>may not open</u> your eyes.

PRACTICE QUIZ

Convert the following verbs / adjectives to describe permission using ~(으)면 안된다.

놀다 to play –> _____ not allowed to/may play

입다 to wear –> _____ not allowed to/may wear

구르다 to roll –> _____ not allowed to/may roll

더럽다 is dirty –> _____ not allowed to/may be dirty

크다 is big –> _____ not allowed to/may be big

ANSWER: 놀면 안된다. / 입으면 안된다. / 구르면 안된다. / 더러우면 안된다다. / 크면 안된다.

149

MP3 ⟨65⟩

Reason

~아/어서 / ~기 때문에

Add ~**아/어서** / ~**기 때문에** to verb / adjective stem to mean "because (of)"

For example,

보다 to see –> **봐**서 ⟨보+아서⟩ OR **보**기 때문에 because I see/watch

e.g.,) 지금 영화를 **봐**서 ⟨보기 때문에⟩, 통화 할 수 없다.

I can't talk on the phone now because I'm watching a movie now.

날다 to fly–> **날**아서 OR **날**기 때문에 because (subject) fly/flies

e.g.,) 모기는 너무 빨리 **날**아서 ⟨날기 때문에⟩, 잡기 힘들다.

Mosquitoes are difficult to catch because they fly too fast.

먹다 to eat –> **먹**어서 OR **먹**기 때문에 because (subject) eat(s)

e.g.,) 나는 화가 나면 너무 많이 **먹**어서 ⟨먹기 때문에⟩, 조심해야 한다.

I need to be careful because I eat too much when I get angry.

예쁘다 is pretty –> **예뻐**서 OR **예쁘**기 때문에 because (subject) is/are/am pretty

e.g.,) 그녀는 **예뻐**서 ⟨예쁘기 때문에⟩, 모두가 부러워한다.

Everybody is envious because she is pretty.

맵다 is spicy –> **매워**서 ⟨매+우어서= 매워서 *irregular conjugation⟩ OR **맵**기 때문에

because (food) is spicy

e.g.,) 음식이 **매워**서 ⟨맵기 때문에⟩, 물을 많이 마셨다.

(Subject) drank a lot of water because the food is spicy.

150

(Subject) can see the starts <u>because it's dark</u>.

PRACTICE QUIZ

Add ~아서/어서/~기 때문에 to verb / adjective stems to mean "because (of)".

놀다 to play -> _____ because (subject) play

입다 to wear -> _____ because (subject) wear

구르다 to roll -> _____ because (subject) roll

더럽다 is dirty -> _____ because (subject) is dirty

크다 is big -> _____ because (subject) is big

ANSWER: 놀기 때문에 or 놀아서 / 입기 때문에 or 입어서 / 구르기 때문에 or 굴러서 / 더럽기 때문에 or 더러워서 / 크기 때문에 or 커서.

 MP3 ⟨66⟩

Possibility

~ㄹ/을 수 있다 / ~ㄹ/을 수 없다

Add ~ㄹ/을 수 있다 to verb / adjective stem to mean "it's possible to" = "can (be)"

For example,

보다 to see –> **볼** 수 있다. It's possible to see (it). = (Subject) can see (it).

날다 to fly–> **날** 수 있다. It's possible to fly. = (Subject) can fly.

먹다 to eat –> **먹**을 수 있다. It's possible to eat. = (Subject) can eat.

예쁘다 is pretty –> **예쁠** 수 있다. It's possible to be pretty. = (Subject) can be pretty.

맵다 is spicy –> **매울** 수 있다 (*irregular conjugation) It's possible for (food) to be spicy. = It can be spicy.

할 수 있다!

(하다 + ㄹ 수 있다 = 할 수 있다)

I can do it!

PRACTICE QUIZ

Convert the following verbs / adjectives to describe possibility using ~ㄹ/을 수 있다.

놀다 to play –> _____ can play

입다 to wear –> _____ can wear

구르다 to roll –> _____ can roll

더럽다 is dirty –> _____ can be dirty

크다 is big –> _____ can be big

ANSWER: 놀 수 있다. / 입을 수 있다. / 구를 수 있다. / 더러울 수 있다. / 클 수 있다.

Conversely, add **~르/을 수 없다** to verb / adjective stem to mean "it's not possible to" = "can't (be)"

For example,

보다 to see –> **볼 <u>수 없다</u>**. It's not possible to see (it). = (Subject) can't see (it).

날다 to fly–> **날 <u>수 없다</u>**. It's not possible to fly. = (Subject) can't fly.

먹다 to eat –> **먹을 <u>수 없다</u>**. It's not possible to eat. = (Subject) can't eat.

예쁘다 is pretty –> **예쁠 <u>수 없다</u>**. It's not possible to be pretty. = (Subject) can't be pretty.

맵다 is spicy –> **매울 <u>수 없다</u>** (*irregular conjugation) It's not possible for (food) to be spicy. = It can't be spicy.

할 <u>수 없다</u>!

(**하다** + <u>르 수 없다</u> = **할 <u>수 없다</u>**)

I can't do it!

PRACTICE QUIZ

Convert the following verbs / adjectives to describe possibility using **~르/을 수 없다**.

놀다 to play –> _____ can't play

입다 to wear –> _____ can't wear

구르다 to roll –> _____ can't roll

더럽다 is dirty –> _____ can't be dirty

크다 is big –> _____ can't be big

ANSWER: 놀 수 없다. / 입을 수 없다. / 구를 수 없다. / 더러울 수 없다. / 클 수 없다.

Despite

~지만

Add ~지만 to verb / adjective stem to mean "despite/though"

For example,

보다 to see –> 보지만 despite/though (subject) see(s)/watches,

e.g., 영화를 보지만, 공부 할 수 있다. <u>Though</u> I <u>watch</u> a movie, I can study.

날다 to fly–> 날지만 despite/though (subject) fly/flies,

e.g., 모기는 빨리 날지만, 잡을 수 있다. <u>Though</u> mosquitoes <u>fly</u> fast, (I) can catch it.

먹다 to eat –> 먹지만 despite/though (subject) eat(s),

e.g., 나는 많이 먹지만, 날씬하다. <u>Though</u> I <u>eat</u> a lot, I am thin

예쁘다 is pretty –> 예쁘지만 despite/though (subject) is/am/are pretty,

e.g., 장미꽃은 예쁘지만, 가시가 있다. <u>Though</u> roses <u>are pretty</u>, they have thorns.

맵다 is spicy –> 맵지만 despite/though (food) is spicy,

e.g., 김치는 맵지만, 건강에 좋다. <u>Though</u> kimchi <u>is spicy</u>, it's good for health.

Though the weather is cold, it feels good.　　Though ornaments are pretty, they are complicated.

PRACTICE QUIZ

Add ~지만 to verb / adjective stems to mean "despite/though".

놀다 to play -> _____ despite/though (subject) play

입다 to wear -> _____ despite/though (subject) wear

구르다 to roll -> _____ despite/though (subject) roll

더럽다 is dirty -> _____ despite/though (subject) is/am/are dirty

크다 is big -> _____ despite/though (subject) is/am/are big

ANSWER: 놀지만 / 입지만 / 구르지만 / 더럽지만 / 크지만

Quote

~(ㄴ/는)다고 / ~았/었다고 / ~ㄹ 거라고

Add ~(ㄴ/는다고) to verb / adjective stem to mean "says that (subject) + action present"

Add ~았/었다고 to verb / adjective stem to mean "says that (subject) + action past"

Add ~ㄹ 거라고 to verb / adjective stem to mean "says that (subject) + action future"

보다 to see –> 본다고 said/heard that (subject) see(s) / 보았다고 saw / 볼 거라고 will see/watch

e.g.,) 철수가 영화를 본다고 / 보았다고 / 볼 거라고 말했다.

Cheol–su said that he is watching / watched / will watch a movie.

날다 to fly–> 난다고 said/heard that (subject) fly/flies / 날았다고 flew / 날 거라고 will fly

e.g.,) 독수리가 하늘을 난다고 / 날았다고 / 날 거라고 들었다.

I heard that the eagle is flying/ flew / will fly in the sky.

먹다 to eat –> 먹는다고 said/heard that (subject) eat(s) / 먹었다고 ate / 먹을 거라고 will eat

e.g.,) 영희가 식탁 위의 햄버거를 먹는다고 / 먹었다고 / 먹을 거라고 말했다.

Young–hee said that she is eating / ate / will eat the hamburger on the dining table.

예쁘다 is pretty –> 예쁘다고 said/heard that (subject) is pretty / 예뻤다고 was pretty

/ 예쁠 거라고 will be pretty

e.g.,) 새로 나온 자동차가 예쁘다고 / 예뻤다고 / 예쁠 거라고 들었다.

I heard that the newly debuted car is pretty / was pretty / will be pretty.

맵다 is spicy –> 맵다고 (not 맵는다고) said/heard that (food) is spicy / 매웠다고 was spicy

/ 매울 거라고 will be spicy

e.g.,) 김치 라면이 맵다고 / 매웠다고 / 매울 거라고 들었다.

I heard that the kimchi ramyon is spicy/ was spicy / will be spicy.

I heard that oppa liked me.

And he said that
he still likes me now!

And, he said that
he will continue to like me!

PRACTICE QUIZ

Covert each of the following verbs / adjectives ~(ㄴ/는)다고 / ~았/었다고 / ~ㄹ 거라고 to quote something in
action present / action past / action future forms. Write underneath each sentence.

놀다 to play

said that (subject) plays / said that (subject) played / said that (subject) will play

더럽다 is dirty

said that (subject) is dirty / said that (subject) was dirty / said that (subject) will be dirty

ANSWER: 논다고 말했다. 놀았다고 말했다. 놀 거라고 말했다..
입는다고 들었다. 입었다고 들었다. 입을 거라고 들었다.
더럽다고 들었다. 더러웠다고 들었다. 더러울 거라고 들었다.

Guess

~ㄹ/을 것 같다 / ~ㄴ/은 것 같다 / ~었던 것 같다

Add ~ㄹ/을 것 같다 to verb / adjective stem to mean "seems like (subject) will (be)"

Add ~ㄴ/은 것 같다 to verb stem to mean "seems like (subject) did"

* for adjectives, add ~었던 것 같다 to the stem to mean "think (subject) was"

보다 to see -> **볼** 것 같다 seems like (subject) will see/watch / **본** 것 같다 seems like (subject) saw/watched

e.g.,) 영희와 철수가 영화를 **볼** 것 같다 / **본** 것 같다.

It <u>seems like</u> Young-hee and Cheol-su <u>will watch</u> / <u>watched</u> a movie.

날다 to fly-> **날** 것 같다 seems like (subject) will fly / **난** 것 같다 seems like (subject) flew

e.g.,) 독수리가 하늘을 **날** 것 같다 / **난** 것 같다.

It <u>seems like</u> the eagle <u>will fly</u> / <u>flew</u> in the sky.

먹다 to eat -> **먹을** 것 같다 seems like (subject) will eat / **먹은 것 같다** seems like (subject) ate

e.g.,) 소희가 식탁 위의 햄버거를 **먹을** 것 같다 / **먹은** 것 같다.

It <u>seems like</u> Sohee <u>will eat</u> / <u>ate</u> the hamburger on the dining table.

예쁘다 is pretty -> **예쁠** 것 같다 seems like (subject) will be pretty / **예뻤던 것 같다** seems pretty

e.g.,) 새로 나온 자동차가 **예쁠** 것 같다 / **예뻤던** 것 같다.

ADJ It <u>seems like</u> the newly debuted car <u>will be pretty</u> /I <u>think</u> the newly debuted car <u>was pretty</u>.

맵다 is spicy -> **매울** 것 같다 seems like (food) will be spicy / **매웠던 것 같다** seems like (food) is spicy

e.g.,) 김치가 **매울** 것 같다 / **매웠던** 것 같다.

It <u>seems like</u> kimchi <u>will be spicy</u> / It <u>think</u> kimchi <u>was spicy</u>.

성공할 것 같아?

성공한 것 같아요!

Does it <u>seem like</u> I <u>will succeed</u>?

It <u>seems like</u> you <u>succeeded</u>!

한국은 더울 것 같아요?

응! 많이 더웠던 것 같다!

ADJ Does it <u>seem like</u> Korea <u>will be hot</u>?

Yup! I <u>think</u> Korea was <u>hot!</u>

PRACTICE QUIZ

Add ~ㄹ/을 것 같다 or ~ㄴ/은 것 같다 / ~었던 것 같다 (adj) to mean "seems like~ will (be)" or "seems like ~ did" or "seems like ~ was".

놀다 to play

_____ seems like (subject) will play

_____ seems like (subject) played

입다 to wear

_____ seems like (subject) will wear

_____ seems like (subject) wore

더럽다 is dirty

_____ seems like (subject) will be dirty

_____ think (subject) was dirty

크다 is big

_____ seems like (subject) will be big

_____ think (subject) was big

ANSWER: 놀 것 같다. 논 것 같다 / 입을 것 같다. / 입은 것 같다. / 더러울 것 같다. / 더러웠던 것 같다. / 클 것 같다. / 컸던 것 같다.

Condition / If

~(으)면, ~(ㄴ/는) 다면

Add ~(으)면, ~ㄴ/는다면 to verb / adjective stem to mean "if ~ "

For example,

보다 to see –> 보면 or 본다면 if I see/watch

e.g.,) 금요일에 영화를 보면 / 본다면 어때요? How is it if we watch a movie on Friday?

날다 to fly–> 날면 / 난다면 if (subject) fly/flies

e.g.,) 독수리가 하늘을 날면 / 난다면? What if the eagle flies in the sky?

먹다 to eat –> 먹으면 / 먹는다면 if (subject) eat(s)

e.g.,) 내가 이 햄버거를 먹으면 / 먹는다면, 살 찔까? If I eat this hamburger, would I get fat?

예쁘다 is pretty –> 예쁘면 / 예쁘다면 if pretty

e.g.,) 자동차 디자인이 예쁘면 / 예쁘다면, 비쌀까? If the car design is pretty, would it be expensive?

맵다 is spicy –> 매우면 / 맵다면 if spicy

e.g.,) 너무 매우면 / 맵다면, 물을 좀 마셔요. If too spicy, drink some water.

If you don't know the answer,   You will know the answer if you study hard!

PRACTICE QUIZ

Convert the following into conditional form by using either ~(으)면, or ~(ㄴ/는) 다면 of your choice.

놀다 to play -> _____ if (subject) play(s)

입다 to wear -> _____ if (subject) wear(s)

구르다 to roll -> _____ if (subject) roll(s)

더럽다 is dirty -> _____ if (subject) is dirty

크다 is big -> _____ if (subject) is big

ANSWER: 놀면 or 논다면 / 입으면 or 입는다면 / 구르면 or 구른다면 / 더러우면 or 더럽다면 / 크면 or 크다면

At The Same Time

~(으)면서 / ~며

Add ~(으)면서 / ~며 to verb / adjective stem to mean "while ~ ing"

For example,

보다 to see –> **보면서** or **보며** while seeing / watching

e.g.,) 영화를 **보면서** / **보며** 김밥을 먹었다.

(I) ate kimbap <u>while watching</u> a movie.

날다 to fly–> **날면서** / **날며** while flying

e.g.,) 독수리가 하늘을 **날면서** / **날며** 사냥을 했다.

The eagle hunted <u>while flying</u> in the sky.

먹다 to eat –> **먹으면서** / **먹으며** while eating

e.g.,) 라면을 **먹으면서** / **먹으며** 공부했다.

I studied <u>while eating</u> ramyon.

예쁘다 is pretty –> **예쁘면서** / **예쁘며** while being pretty

e.g.,) 이 옷은 **예쁘면서** / **예쁘며** 가격도 싸다.

This dress is cheap <u>while it's pretty</u>. = This dress is cheap. <u>At the same time it's pretty.</u>

맵다 is spicy –> **매우면서** / **매우며** while being spicy

e.g.,) 김치는 **매우면서** / **매우며**, 새콤하다.

Kimchi is sour <u>while it's spicy</u>. = Kimchi is sour. <u>At the same time it's spicy.</u>

PRACTICE QUIZ

Convert the following into present continuous using either ~(으)면서, or ~며 of your choice.

놀다 to play –> _____ while playing

입다 to wear –> _____ while giving

구르다 to roll –> _____ while rolling

더럽다 is dirty –> _____ while being dirty

크다 is big –> _____ while being big

ANSWER: 놀면서 or 놀며 / 입으면서 or 입으며 / 구르면서 or 구르며 / 더러우면서 or 더러우며 / 크면서 or 크며

Nearly / Almost

~ㄹ/을 뻔 했다

Add ~ㄹ/을 뻔 했다 to verb stem to mean "nearly / almost (did)"

to adjective stem to mean "would/could have been"

For example,

보다 to see -> 볼 뻔 했다 almost / nearly saw/watched (it)

e.g.,) 재미 없는 영화를 끝까지 볼 뻔 했다. (I) <u>almost watched</u> the boring movie to the end.

날다 to fly-> 날 뻔 했다 almost flew

e.g.,) 독수리가 놀라서 하늘로 날 뻔 했다. The eagle almost flew into the sky in surprise.

먹다 to eat -> 먹을 뻔 했다 almost / nearly ate

e.g.,) 상한 음식을 먹을 뻔 했다. I almost ate spoiled food.

예쁘다 is pretty -> 예쁠 뻔 했다 might have been pretty

e.g.,) 장식이 있으면 예쁠 뻔 했다. It might have been pretty if it had an ornament.

맵다 is spicy -> 매울 뻔 했다 might have been spicy

e.g.,) 고추장을 넣었으면 매울 뻔 했다. It might have been spicy if I put gochujang.

I almost died!

I almost fell asleep!

PRACTICE QUIZ

Add ~르/을 뻔 했다 to the following verb stems to mean "nearly / almost (did)"
and adjective stems to mean "would / could have been".

놀다 to play –> _____ nearly / almost played.

입다 to wear –> _____ nearly / almost wore (clothes).

구르다 to roll –> _____ nearly / almost rolled.

더럽다 is dirty –> _____ would / could have been dirty.

크다 is big –> _____ would / could have been big.

ANSWER: 놀 뻔 했다. / 입을 뻔 했다. / 구를 뻔 했다. / 더러울 뻔 했다. / 클 뻔 했다.

Make / Let / Force

~게 하다 / ~게 해 주다 / ~게 만들다

Add ~게 하다 to verb stem to mean "make (subject) do/be"

Add ~게 해 주다 to verb stem to mean "let (subject) do/be"

Add ~게 만들다 to verb stem to mean "force (subject) to do/be"

For example,

보다 to see -> 보게 하다 make (subject) see/watch 보게 해 주다 let (subject) see/watch

보게 만들다 force (subject) to see/watch

e.g.,) 선생님이 학생들이 공포영화를 보게 하다 / 보게 해 주다 / 보게 만들다

The teacher makes / let / force the students (to) see a horror movie.

날다 to fly-> 날게 하다 make (subject) fly 날게 해 주다 let (subject) fly

날게 만들다 force (subject) to fly

e.g.,) 독수리가 하늘로 날게 하다 / 날게 해 주다 / 날게 만들다

(I) make / let / force the eagle (to) fly into the sky.

먹다 to eat-> 먹게 하다 make (subject) eat 먹게 해 주다 let (subject) eat 먹게 만들다 force (subject) to eat

e.g.,) 상한 음식을 먹게 하다 / 먹게 해 주다 / 먹게 만들다

(I) make / let / force (subject) (to eat) spoiled food.

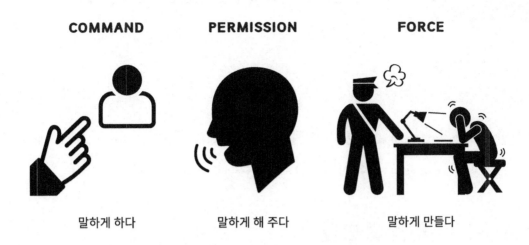

COMMAND	PERMISSION	FORCE
말하게 하다	말하게 해 주다	말하게 만들다

PRACTICE QUIZ

Add ~게 하다 to verb stem to mean "make (subject) do/be"

Add ~게 해 주다 to verb stem to mean "let (subject) do/be"

Add ~게 만들다 to verb stem to mean "force (subject) to do/be"

놀다 to play -> _____ make (subject) play.

_____ let (subject) play.

_____ force (subject) to play.

입다 to wear -> _____ make (subject) wear.

_____ let (subject) wear.

_____ force (subject) to wear.

화나다 is angry -> _____ make (subject) be angry.

_____ let (subject) be angry.

_____ force (subject) to be angry.

ANSWER: 놀게 하다. 놀게 해 주다. 놀게 만들다. / 입게 하다. 입게 해 주다. 입게 만들다. / 화나게 하다. 화나게 해 주다. 화나게 만들다.

 **OTHER COMMON EXPRESSIONS**

As soon as ~자마자

먹다 – 먹<u>자마자</u> as soon as (you) eat 먹<u>자마자</u> 자면 안된다. It's not okay to sleep as soon as you eat.

보다 – 보<u>자마자</u> as soon as (you) see 보<u>자마자</u> 전화해! Call me as soon as you see (this)!

To know how to do ~ㄹ/을 줄 안다

먹다 – 먹<u>을 줄 안다</u> know how to eat 나도 랍스터 먹<u>을 줄 안다</u>. I know how to eat a lobster, too.

보다 – 볼 <u>줄 안다</u> know how to see 지도를 볼 <u>줄 안다</u>. (I) know how to see (read) a map.

Decide to ~기로 하다

먹다 – 먹<u>기로 하다</u> decide to eat 건강하게 먹<u>기로 하다</u>. (I) decide to eat healthy.

보다 – 보<u>기로 하다</u> decide to see 영화를 함께 보<u>기로 하다</u>. (They) decide to see a movie together.

Asking for approval ~죠?

먹다 – 먹<u>죠</u>? eat, don't you?/right? 어린이들이 햄버거 많이 먹<u>죠</u>? Kids eat lots of hamburgers, right?

보다 – 보<u>죠</u>? see/watch, don't you?/right? 영화 많이 보<u>죠</u>? (You) watch a lot of movies, don't you?

예쁘다 – 예쁘<u>죠</u>? pretty, isn't it?/right? 이 인형 예쁘<u>죠</u>? This doll is pretty, isn't it?

맵다 – 맵<u>죠</u>? spicy, isn't it?/right? 이 김치가 많이 맵<u>죠</u>? This kimchi is very spicy, right?

End up doing ~게 되다

먹다 – 먹<u>게 되다</u>. end up eating 매운 김치를 먹<u>게 되다</u>. (I) end up eating spicy kimchi.

보다 – 보<u>게 되다</u>. end up seeing/watching 무서운 영화를 보<u>게 되다</u>. (I) end up watching a scary movie.

In order to ~(으)려면

먹다 – 먹으려면 in order to eat 밥을 먹으려면 손을 씻으세요. In order to eat a meal, please wash hands.

보다 – 보려면 in order to see/watch 미래를 보려면, 책을 읽어라. In order to see the future, read a book.

Worth ~ㄹ/을 만 하다

먹다 – 먹을 만 하다 worth eating 이 음식은 먹을 만 하다. This food is worth eating.

보다 – 볼 만 하다 worth seeing/watching 이 영화는 볼 만 하다. This movie is worth watching.

HONORIFICS

In Korean, there are different levels of speech (casual / formal / honorific), depending on the social hierarchy and the relative relationship between the speaker and the listener.

Common examples of when to use honorifics include:

− Student (Lower Status) to Teacher (Higher Status)
− Intern (Lower Rank) to CEO (Higher Rank)
− Grandson (Lower Age) to Grandpa (Higher Age)
− Public Document / Notice

Usually, between people of same rank/status/age use casual, from lower rank to higher rank formal, and from young to elderly, honorific.

In general, honorifics can be made by using **honorific verbs/predicates** and **honorific nouns.** Let's look at some of the most common examples.

	Korean	Casual	Formal	Honorific
1	읽다 to read	읽다	읽으시다	
	가다 to go	가다	가시다	
2	자다 to sleep	자다	주무시다	
3	있다 to be present	있다	있으시다	계시다
	아프다 is sick	아프다	아프시다	편찮으시다
	배고프다 is hungry	배고프다	배고프시다	시장하시다
4	먹다 to eat	먹다	드시다	잡수시다

As you can see, there are four types of honorific verbs / predicates.

#1 type – Made by adding ~(으)시다 to verb / predicate stem. This is the most common type.

#2 type – Also made by adding ~(으)시다 to verb / predicate stem, but the suffix is different from the base form.

자다 –> 자시다 (x) 주무시다 (o)

You can think of this as irregular types.

#3 type – It follows type **#1**, with a separate word for honorific level.

e.g., 있다 –> 있으시다 (#1 type) –> 계시다 (separate honorific)

아프다 –> 아프시다 (#1 type) –> 편찮으시다 (separate honorific)

배고프다 –> 배고프시다 (#1 type) –> 시장하시다 (separate honorific)

#4 type – It follows the type **#2**, plus a separate word for honorific level.

e.g., 먹다 –> 드시다 (#2 type) –> 잡수시다 (separate honorific)

Now that we looked at the honorific verbs / predicates, let's learn the honorific nouns.

Noun	Casual	Formal	Honorific
이름 name	이름	성함	존함
밥 meal	밥	식사	진지
나이 age	나이		연세
생일 birthday	생일		생신

Like verbs / predicates, there are more than one type for honorific usage.
#1 type is where casual / formal / and honorific levels have separate word for each.
#2 type is where casual and formal share the same word but has a separate word for honorific level.

Now, one very important rule when using honorifics is you never use it for yourself, but only for someone else. Here's an example.

MP3 (76)

> Cheol-su: 선생님, 점심 드셨어요? Teacher, did you eat (= have) lunch?
>
> Teacher: 응. 점심 먹었어. 철수도 점심 먹었니? Yes, I ate lunch. Did you eat lunch, too, Cheol-su?
>
> Cheol-su: 네 선생님. 저도 점심 먹었습니다. Yes, teacher. I also ate (= had a meal) lunch.

Here, you can see that when asking the teacher,
Cheol-su address using the honorific verb 드셨어요 (past tense for 드시다 = 드시+었어요)

Now, notice that the teacher answers by 먹었어, which is the casual form, because using 드셨어요 for yourself is the same as praising yourself, which sounds very awkward. (e.g., "Yes, it is I, the magnificent Joe who had lunch!")

Also, when the teacher asks Cheol-su if he ate, he/she uses casual, 먹었니? because the listener, Cheol-su is younger and is also of lower status than the teacher.

Lastly, Cheol-su answers the teacher using 먹었습니다, which is formal polite past tense of 먹다.

PRACTICE QUIZ

Fill in the blanks by using the appropriate word.

1. 내 친구 영희가 책을 _____ My friend Young-hee reads a book.
   a. 읽는다.   b. 읽으신다.   c. 읽쓰신다.   d. 읽으스신다.

2. 교수님께서 집에 _____ Professor went home.
   a. 갔다.   b. 가었다.   c. 가였었다.   d. 가셨다.

3. 할아버지께서 진지를 _____. Grandpa ate a meal.
   a. 먹으셨다.   b. 드셨다.   c. 잡수셨다.   d. 드시셨다.

4. 공부 열심히 해라! 선생님께서 _____. Study hard! Said the teacher.
   a. 말했었다.   b. 말하셨다.   c. 말씀했다.   d. 말씀하셨다.

ANSWER: 1. a. 읽는다. 2. d. 가셨다. 3. c. 잡수셨다. 4. d. 말씀하셨다.

Match the following verbs / predicates with correct formal / honorific forms.

Casual	Formal	Honorific
Casual	**Formal**	**Honorific**
보다	가시다	
자다	아프시다	
말하다	읽으시다	
읽다	배고프시다	
입다	보시다	편찮으시다
아프다	입으시다	시장하시다
배고프다	노래하시다	잡수시다
가다	드시다	
노래하다	춤추시다	
춤추다	주무시다	
먹다	말씀하시다	

ANSWER:

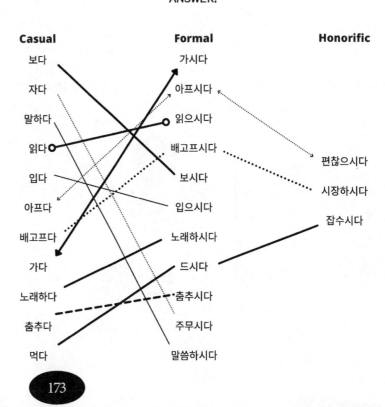

173

All right guys, now that you've learned the basic elements of Korean, you can fine-tune your Korean with our other titles focusing on different subject matter! Here are some of our best selling titles our readers love.

FOR SPEAKING

LET'S SPEAK KOREAN
Learn over 1,400 Expressions Quickly and Easily w/ Pronunciation & Grammar Guide Marks.

Just Listen, Repeat, and Learn!
Each expression comes with free downloadable MP3 files recorded by a native Korean speaker!

GRAMMAR WORKBOOK

LET'S STUDY KOREAN
Complete Practice Workbook for Grammar, Spelling, Vocabulary and Reading Comprehension w/ Over 600 Questions!

WRITING PRACTICE

EASY LEARNING FUNDAMENTAL KOREAN WRITING PRACTICE BOOK

READING COMPREHENSION

ESSENTIAL KOREAN READING COMPREHENSION WORKBOOK
Multi-level practices for Beginners to Advanced

VOCAB BUILDER

KOREAN CULTURE

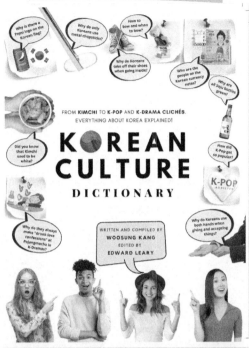

QUICK & EASY KOREAN VOCABULARY

1,000 Essential Words and Phrases w/ Pronunciation Guide

FUN & EASY KOREAN VOCABULARY QUIZ WORKBOOK

Learn **400+** Essential Words w/ Exciting Exercises

K-POP / KOREAN SLANG

THE K-POP DICTIONARY

Fully Understand What Your Favorite Idols Are Saying

500 Essential K-Pop Words & Phrases

Pronunciation Guide

Definitions

Real Life Examples

KOREAN CULTURE DICTIONARY

From Kimchi to K-Pop and K-Drama Cliches. Everything About Korea Explained!

NEW AMPERSAND PUBLISHING
CONNECTING THE WORLD THROUGH LITERATURE

Available in Spanish, Russian, Bulgarian, and Indonesian!

FOR MORE TITLES, PLEASE VIST

NEWAMPERSAND.COM

Printed in Great Britain
by Amazon

28875012R00097